THE
BUSINESS
OF JOY

UNTOLD LESSONS FROM THE PANDEMIC
- WHAT'S NEXT AND HOW TO PREPARE

LISA W. MILLER

CONTENTS

> "When joy is greater than fear, economic recovery begins."
>
> – Lisa W. Miller

DEDICATIONS:

To my husband Ken, my son Andy and
daughters Julia and Catherine
for their support and encouragement throughout my
journey to bring this passion project into a book. Thanks
for always being there for me, no matter what!

To my parents - Jan and Charlie Wyatt.
I am who I am in large part due to them. They were
always supportive in all my endeavors, taught me that
the answer was no unless you ask, let me make my own
mistakes, and encouraged me that 'this too shall pass.'

To the many industry leaders that supported
my Journey Back to Joy work
giving me the confidence that it was making a difference,
especially Barry McGowan, Starlette Johnson, and Sherri Landry.

PREFACE

T HIS IS NOT a self-help book. This is a book about getting back to the business of joy and the invaluable lessons learned that enabled many businesses to not only survive the Covid-19 pandemic but emerge stronger.

As a veteran in the field of consumer strategy and marketing research, I decided to write this book to showcase the dynamic tension between joy and fear and the reasons the Covid economic recovery didn't unfold as planned. It has taken years filled with over 55,000 consumer interviews and countless hours of analysis to unlock the actionable insights to help companies get to the other side of the pandemic - and we are still not entirely where we need to be.

What is joy? Merriam-Webster defines joy as "the emotion evoked by well-being, success, or good fortune or by the prospect of possessing what one desires."[1] Ultimately, joy means different things to different people. This book is about joy - but from a business perspective. Brands that understand and deliver joy will win the hearts, loyalty and share of wallet from their customers and earn the loyalty of their employees.

---

[1] Merriam-Webster. https://www.merriam-webster.com/dictionary/joy

In March of 2020, consumers were told to 'shelter in place' – stay home to help 'flatten the curve' and stop the spread of Covid-19. Many activities were taken away from us in the process. From a consumer behavioral perspective, when we are told we can't do something, it makes us want to do it more. The longer we stayed home in lockdown, the more our pent-up demand for those activities that gave us joy soared. It sparked a fire of appreciation for those activities while also opening us up to new choices we might not otherwise have considered.

After six weeks of sheltering in place, Americans were anxiously anticipating the return to their normal activities. The pressure cooker of demand was ready to be unleashed in May of 2020, and we were hopeful the economic recovery would finally begin. Yet, as the doors across America slowly reopened, it became clear that consumers weren't as ready as they thought to re-engage with the outside world and participate in the activities that had been deemed "non-essential." Whether it was dining out at restaurants, going to movies, attending church, working out at gyms, or going on vacation, many people hesitated and stayed home because the fear of the virus was greater than the joy that they craved.

As I write this, I have to pause to remember that during the pandemic, we were introduced to what I call the "language of Covid." This is such an important part of this story that I created an entire chapter dedicated to it. The word "non-essential" was one of many examples. The number of business categories deemed non-essential was massive: dining rooms in restaurants, movie theaters, cruise ships, gyms, salons, and even churches, just to name a few. As time went one, I would argue we learned that these businesses were indeed essential.

No one could have predicted the sustained deprivation of joy from living our daily lives. It would have been impossible to realize just how essential these "non-essential" activities were to our daily living until the unthinkable happened and the doors were shuttered. This was compounded by the fear of the rapid spread and increased morbidity rates of the virus. Brick-and-mortar businesses swiftly pivoted into survival mode and sought out new ways to engage with their consumers. Sitting back and doing nothing was not an option if there was to be any hope of businesses surviving, let alone thriving.

It was through these experiences we all learned together that business and joy are not necessarily two separate entities. I want to reiterate that this is not a self-help book or a how-to manual, but rather an introspective look at how we can all get back to "the business of joy." While most of the examples in this book are from hospitality or retail leaders, the business lessons learned were felt by every leader whether it be retail, technology, healthcare, transportation, logistics, financial services and more; no business model was left untouched by the pandemic.

Just remember, before we can move forward, we must first look backward. We have to make it a point to listen and learn from the past while reconciling our need for joy against our anxieties and fears. This is a peek into the window of American lives during Covid – the stories of sorrow and fear, as well as joy and resiliency. The journey isn't over, yet we've come a long way.

This is the story of the journey back to joy for America. Whether you were thrilled and excited when communities reopened or you were very hesitant about getting back out there, this book is for you! It reflects the resilience of Americans and the simple truth that many of the shutdown businesses that are reopening their doors are not just functional, but a source of much-needed joy.

I hope we can agree that we all need a bit more joy in our lives and that you will join me on this journey back to joy...

Introduction:
Where were you on Friday,
March 13th, 2020?

I CAN TELL YOU in great detail my first memories of the new coronavirus. It made its appearance in December 2019. In January of the following year, I began hearing about this virus, and how the uncertainties were mounting in China and countries in Europe. In fact, my ophthalmologist, who is Chinese, shared with me stories of friends and family members leaving to escape this virus before the entire country was shut down, which ultimately happened in January 2020. Any way you looked at it, it sounded bad and pretty scary to me.

At the time, it was business as usual for me. As a seasoned consumer marketing research strategist, I collect consumer data then translate that data into insights and recommendations that unlock profitable sales growth for my clients. My team and I were busy conducting marketing research for clients including in-restaurant consumer taste tests – taking extra precautions, of course, trying to do the right thing. But by March, the uncertainties about the virus were mounting as more people were getting sick in the US, specifically, Washington state. Their symptoms were similar to those being experienced in countries where the presence of the virus had been confirmed.

March 11th 11:30 a.m. CST: The World Health Organization declared coronavirus a global pandemic. "We have called every day for countries to take urgent and aggressive action. We have rung the alarm bell loud and clear," said Dr. Tedros Adhanom Ghebreyesus, WHO director-general. He continued, "This is not just a public health crisis, it is a crisis that will touch every sector – so every sector and every individual must be involved in the fight."[2] At that moment, there were 118,000 cases in 114 countries, yet 90% were concentrated in just four countries.

With that announcement, the US stock market plummeted over 1,400 points by the end of day, entering the first bear market in 11 years.

March 11th 7:00 p.m. CST: Later that evening, as a Dallasite, I was watching the Dallas Mavericks basketball game in a sold-out and packed stadium with over 20,000 fans when during the game, Mark Cuban (the owner of the team) was handed a phone by a gentleman in a gray suit and proceeded to read the message. Then… his jaw dropped and he jolted back in his seat, shaking his head in shock – the NBA had just "suspended" their season until further notice "in an abundance of caution" after a Utah Jazz player had tested positive for the coronavirus. From that day forward, there was a domino effect of unprecedented closures across the country and around the world.

The phrase "in an abundance of caution" and others like it would soon become the norm. It was the beginning of the fear and anxiety that we would endure not for days, weeks, or months, but years.

That same day, we learned that actors Tom and Rita Hanks had contracted Covid-19 in Australia and were gravely ill. This was getting real, very real.

---

[2] WHO Director-General's opening remarks at the media briefing on COVID-19 - 11 March 2020
https://www.who.int/director-general/speeches/detail/who-director-general-s-opening-remarks-at-the-media-briefing-on-covid-19---11-march-2020

March 11th 8:00 p.m. CST: President Donald J. Trump announced that he was implementing a 30-day travel ban to the U.S. from European countries, except from the UK. As he put it, it was a "strong but necessary action to protect the health and wellbeing of all Americans." [3]

March 13th: President Trump announced that, "to unleash the full power of the federal government," he was declaring a national emergency.[4] The declaration instructed states to ramp up emergency preparedness plans. The US was moving into a lockdown with the stroke of a pen. Yes, this declaration was on Friday the 13th.

Immediately, my consulting business, like many other businesses, came to a screeching halt. At first, meetings were being canceled as clients were scrambling. Eventually, projects were being canceled left and right. As a small business owner, I found it surreal, to say the least. I even had several clients tell me, "Lisa, we're sorry, we just can't pay you right now." That was from long-standing clients who were not only my clients, but also my friends. We worked together to have them pay what they could when they could, and eventually my clients did get caught up on paying me, but it wasn't until six to nine months later.

Many clients had been furloughed, yet those who kept their jobs went into survival mode. With skeleton staff and budgets slashed, there was neither time nor energy to look up and think about what was coming next from a consumer viewpoint.

And so began my journey to help businesses get back on their feet to get to the other side of the pandemic.

---

[3] The White House. "Remarks by President Trump in Address to the Nation –," n.d. https://trumpwhitehouse.archives.gov/briefings-statements/remarks-president-trump-address-nation/.

[4] The White House. "Proclamation on Declaring a National Emergency Concerning the Novel Coronavirus Disease (COVID-19) Outbreak –," n.d. https://trumpwhitehouse.archives.gov/presidential-actions/proclamation-declaring-national-emergency-concerning-novel-coronavirus-disease-covid-19-outbreak/.

Ask yourself, what do you remember about those early days of the pandemic? What were you doing and how were you feeling?

As part of my journey, I spoke with countless restaurant industry leaders on a regular basis to share my insights to help and, just as importantly, gauge what they were feeling and seeing. As part of this book, we will hear some of their stories.

What were a few of their earliest memories?

Let's start with Anita Adams, CEO of Black Bear Diner, a regional chain based in Reading, California. Anita had been with Black Bear Diner as CFO since 2017, promoted to president in 2019, and had just taken the reins as CEO in January 2020.

She recalled that in late February and early March, much of her team's attention and focus were on finalizing the plans for their annual general manager conference, scheduled for March 6th in Hawaii. This meaningful tradition is where they come together with partners to celebrate. Yet, Anita confided, "The pandemic was unfolding and there was this element of just feeling surreal and having to pivot to these 'go, no-go' meetings about the conference."

On March 1st, the Sunday before the conference should have started, she and her leadership team decided to cancel the conference, much to the disappointment of their franchise partners. "I sent out an email canceling the conference. For me, I think it was that real moment of recognition about the severity, and none of us had ever been through anything like this."

She shared that inwardly, she hoped she had made the wrong decision in canceling that conference, something leaders rarely contemplate. She mentioned, "It was that kind of a moment, right?" On March 5th, just one day before the conference was to have begun, the headlines were dominated by the cruise ship stuck in the waters of San Francisco – a ship sailing from Hawaii with dozens of passengers presenting Covid-like symptoms. Clearly, Anita had made a tough call, but it turned out to be the right one. She continued, "But then roll it forward, and one and a half weeks later, we're taking down all of our diners. I think back on the 'what if.' What if we had all been stranded in Hawaii and had to deal with all the closures from there?"

Anita continued, "I think your focus on finding the joy through all of this is just a good way to frame it. There was so much tragedy, yet there was goodness. I think it was an evaluation for all of us on what matters and the people that matter in our life."

Barry McGowan, CEO of Fogo de Chão, and I discussed that after restaurants were forced to close by government mandates, there were doomsday predictions that the industry would not survive. These predictions suggested that between 50% and 85% of restaurants would permanently shutter. Thankfully, we knew then as we do today, that was never going to happen.

Barry recalled, "We anticipated having to close." Yet, he went on to explain that even before the mandated closures, "The progression was rapid, and the impact was severe. Remember, you're down ten percent, twenty percent, thirty percent. It's pretty scary. You are going from millions of dollars a day to thousands of dollars. You're having to react. It was almost like this big ball rolling down a hill. We just kept staying in front of it all the way to the end of the hill."

New channels of communication had to be opened. No longer would the weekly email be sufficient. They moved all general manager communications to WhatsApp and named the group "Fogo-mundo." Barry and his team stayed open until the very last possible day – when the government said restaurants could no longer serve anyone. "We stretched it out as long as we could. Then, we just had to shut the doors. The next day I was in the office. It was just shocking. And the ramp-up was even more challenging because every municipality was different." Barry guided his general managers to seat guests where they could, putting 'reserved' signs on tables where they couldn't seat. Remember, back then, many restaurants removed furniture based on seating capacities. Fogo didn't. They focused on serving the customers and paid attention locally to the ever-changing mandates.

During many calls, Barry inspired his team to look up beyond the current situation. "I wanted to remind everybody that every pandemic has ended, so this will end too. We just don't know when. So, let's focus beyond the pandemic. Let's focus on joy and hospitality."

THERE WAS NO PLAYBOOK FOR THIS

"When the world pushed pause, we pushed play"

– Pastor Arthur Jones

THE PATH TO get where I am today has been a winding road with a few speed bumps along the way. As a child growing up in Texas, my parents always taught me, "The answer is no, unless you ask." It's a life lesson I've shared with my own children. It seems so simple, yet looking back, that one little statement shaped many facets of my own life, including my career. I think it created a fire in my belly and the insatiable curiosity to ask a lot of questions, probably much to the chagrin of my parents when I was a kid.

With a marketing degree from Southern Methodist University, I cut my teeth in the business world working for an advertising agency on the account of one of the most beloved American icons – Quaker Oats. I always knew that I loved math and statistics. Yet, working at an agency, I learned how much I deeply enjoyed understanding consumer needs and wants, and the translation of that into a creative advertising expression and stories.

1

I love being in the deep weeds of the data, but what I love even more is finding the story. Those skills were invaluable as I moved to the client side at Frito-Lay/PepsiCo and then Brinker International. In 2008, I took the plunge and started my own business. It's now over a decade later and I haven't looked back.

Over the course of time, I have learned a thing or two about the objective interpretation of data and how to use it to garner important insights. While working with franchisees from both Applebee's and IHOP, this approach earned me the nickname of Switzerland. Switzerland is notoriously neutral, and so are my insights. I present the voice of the consumer: no sugar coating, no hidden agenda, no biases, just the facts. Whether good news or bad news, my independent voice assures my clients that I have their best interest in mind. We were all on the same team – no gotcha moments, just insights to help them grow. The same holds true for this book.

1.   THE SITUATION: A SURREAL NEW REALITY

In my conversations with John Cywinski, President of Applebee's, we chatted about how unfathomable the pandemic was: "What if I was pitching a new movie and told you, I've got this great Hollywood script? Imagine if I said four or five years ago, 'Lisa, there's gonna come a point in time where every American is going to be wearing a mask in public, schools are going to be closed and public sporting events — high school, college, professional — are going to be shut down. Or if they exist at all, they're going to be zero spectators.'" He continued, "'Imagine that the airlines are going to be impacted, that hotels will be closed, and cruise lines will be closed, and restaurants will be closed.' You would have said it's too far-fetched a Hollywood script to publish."

Unfortunately, that far-fetched surreal story became real, very real. It was exactly what happened, but there was no script and no playbook for this.

New York City

Radio City Music Hall was silent. Photo courtesy of John Eales

Dallas Love Field Airport

No travelers in sight at Love Field Airport. Photo by Lisa W. Miller

Without a doubt, one of the most challenging moments of my career was early in the pandemic. My clients were in survival mode and keeping their doors open was the main goal every day. There was no roadmap for operators or marketers. There was so much free data out there to help, but I wasn't convinced that the right questions were being asked. As both a researcher and participant in the pandemic, I knew I could help my clients learn from the events we were living through. There are best practices to glean that might not have been useful in the moment but will undoubtedly be of value when planning to make sure a business disruption like this never happens again.

But during a global pandemic, looking backward in the rearview mirror to see what strategies had worked in the past wasn't going to be helpful to get businesses back on their feet. Confounding this issue was the bombardment of seemingly endless and conflicting scientific and consumer data, creating more uncertainty in a time and place where stability was what was really needed.

It was all day, every day just to survive. Who could think about what might come tomorrow? It was mentally and physically exhausting to navigate the complicated restrictions imposed by state and local municipalities, case counts, hospitalizations, PPP, PPE, employee safety, and more.

2. THE CHALLENGE: MEASURING THE SEEMINGLY UNMEASURABLE

As a consumer insights strategist and researcher who supports the restaurant and hospitality industries, the challenge was figuring out how to help my clients as they were struggling to navigate these murky waters. My career and life revolve around gathering data and interpreting it in a meaningful way, but at the end of the day, the world didn't need more data. We have enough of that! In fact, someone once told me that any good insight must be a healthy mix of broccoli and Häagen-Dazs, data being the former and inspirational stories the latter.

Businesses needed insights, not just data, if they were going to make it to the other side of the pandemic. There were too many questions and not enough answers, and the information found in the mainstream news was often contradictory.

How long would it be before the doors opened again?

What would happen when they did open?

What would the consumer reentry curve look like?

Who would lead the economic recovery and venture out first?

What would the new cost of doing business be?

Reality quickly set in. Identifying the questions that I needed to ask was the easy part. Making sense of what to do next was definitely more challenging. Let me tell you, trying to measure intangibles like joy and fear in a global pandemic is no easy task. How could one measure and predict what would happen when the months or years of pent-up demand were finally unleashed?

That's where I came in. As a consumer insights strategist, I was interested in how this sentiment would translate to our consumption behaviors. My craft is the art of storytelling through consumer insights grounded in hard data. My goal line has always been clear: to make complex data and analysis simple and easy to understand for the board of directors and senior executive teams so that they can act and drive growth within their respective organizations.

For decades, we've been living in a world of too much data and not enough insights. Covid changed the rules of engagement for everything, including marketing research. How questions were asked needed to change. More importantly, how we interpret data also needed to change. The biggest question I had from the very beginning was:

How can we dig deep into the data while also seeing the big picture?

It's like seeing the individual puzzle pieces, but also being able to imagine what the final picture would look like.

Many of us like to do puzzles, especially jigsaw puzzles. They are challenging but the answer is known – it's right in front of us on the box to use as a guide. All we have to do is find the pieces and match them up. But Covid was a new kind of challenging puzzle. Just when we began to see the picture, it changed. It became unpredictable. But was it really?

3.   THE SPARK: WHEN JOY WAS GREATER THAN FEAR, THE ECONOMIC RECOVERY WOULD BEGIN

I was in search of something powerful yet fundamental. For my efforts to be meaningful, the insights needed to add structure to the chaos. Adding clarity and predictability to the uncertainty would allow others to see the same thing I did. My aha moment realization – the only path forward would be through joy, not fear. That is when the spark and the connection happened for me to start this work.

My thesis was that when joy was greater than fear, the economic recovery would begin. When that happened, consumers would finally have the confidence to venture back out. And so it began – the passion project called the Journey Back to Joy research was born. As I write, over two years later, with more than 50 waves of research and over 50,000 consumer surveys, I have been tracking the consumer re-entry and how consumers and business emerged on the other side of this. As consumers lived through the pandemic and began their journey back to joy, clear patterns emerged in the data that I will share in this book.

LESSONS LEARNED
CREATING A NEW PLAYBOOK

Hindsight shows us that there were signals missed and opportunities for things to have been done differently during the pandemic. At the core, my intent is to capture the humanity and the lessons learned from our collective experiences.

The soul of doing great research work comes from the interpretation – connecting the dots, creating the stories, and anticipating what's next. While numbers and data are at the heart of any consumer research project, data without insights are cold, sterile, and inactive.

1. By the time you finish reading this book, I hope that you feel better prepared with insights, data, and even a playbook in case this were to ever happen again. By the way, I hope we can all agree that we don't ever want to go through this again!
2. You will learn about the heart-wrenching unintended consequences that we should absolutely never repeat and some gifts from the pandemic we should tightly embrace.
3. It's not "what we did" during the pandemic that's important, but more "how we did it" so we can scale it moving forward. I hope to inspire companies to act and create massive change and growth for years to come.
4. Last, but certainly not least, I hope you will have fun strolling down memory lane with me, remembering some of the heartwarming stories as well as the outrageously funny and sometimes ridiculous things that happened along the way. You might even mumble, "Did that really happen? I can't believe we really did that!" Trust me on this one; I hear this all the time as I share stories of "the Covid pandemic era."

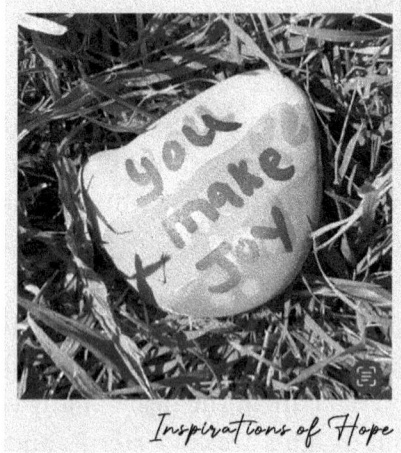

Inspirations of hope on hand painted rocks – Photo by Lisa W. Miller

Zoom meeting protocols

SURVIVE.
SUSTAIN. GROW.

"This simplification of just how do I survive, how do I sustain, then how do I grow my business? It just really crystallizes what the choices are."

– Ricky Richardson, CEO, Eggs Up Grill

I F YOU THINK about the normal life cycle for a business, this chapter title might not sound too far off. Twenty percent of new businesses do not survive their first two years, according to the Bureau of Labor Statistics, and 45% do not last five years. Yet, when the doors are completely closed, and a pandemic lingers on for two-plus years, it's hard for any company — whether new or mature — to survive, let alone sustain and grow.

Let me take you back to March of 2020 when leaders turned sheer chaos and ambiguity into structure, clarity, and purpose to the best of their abilities.

SURVIVE.

1. IN AN INSTANT, THINGS CHANGED

As I alluded to earlier, I wanted to include stories from restaurant leaders to shed light on how the industry came out stronger on the other side of the most challenging season in recent history. One of my interviews was with Ricky Richardson, CEO of Eggs Up Grill, a breakfast and lunch franchise with locations across the Southeast. During our discussion, Ricky described his early pandemic days in three simple words: "Survive. Sustain. Grow." Throughout my many CEO interviews, the words might have been different, but the essence was the same.

As decisions and mandates came down from both the federal and state levels, many businesses immediately went into survival mode. There was no clarity about what the pandemic would bring or how long it would last. If you think back to March of 2020, uncertainty quickly escalated into anxiousness and fear.

With each passing day, federal and state governments deemed more industries "non-essential," causing them to close their doors. It's no surprise that brick-and-mortar retailers without an online presence or drive-thru facilities were some of the businesses most severely affected.

Yet as the closures became the new reality, businesses were jolted out of autopilot with no playbook. No matter how large or small a business might have been or the amount of resources they possessed, in the blink of an eye they were all put on a level playing field, where merely keeping the lights on became the priority.

During my interview with Ricky Richardson, he shared with me that his private equity firm told him early on in the pandemic to do whatever was necessary to survive. Having such a vote of confidence empowered Ricky and his team to make decisions and take risks many other companies might have been afraid of or lacked the resources to undertake.

In a true survival mindset, the primary goal for Eggs Up Grill was not to lose any of its franchises. To accomplish this, they took steps to waive as many of their financial obligations as possible or defer them to future dates, as many other franchisors did. They renegotiated balances owed to suppliers and structured delayed payment schedules to increase liquidity when it was needed the most. Ricky was proud to share that all of his franchisees weathered the storm and survived the pandemic!

Tobin Ellis, founder and principal of Studio Barmagic, a hospitality experience design firm, also went into survival mode. He is a former bartender. Not just any bartender mind you, but a six-time national bartending champion with a lot of flair, who is also a hospitality designer and operations consultant. Tobin will chime in at the end and say, "mostly bartender, at heart."

He recalled, "It was hard. I saw my industry collapsing in a week, and I just felt helpless. I had nothing to do because my business flatlined immediately." He continued with a story he learned from a fellow bartender, "When the sh#t hits the fan, everyone reverts back to their comfort zone." So, that's exactly what Tobin did. He reverted back to his ability to produce large volumes of data, synthesize it, and get it out quickly. In record time he created the Hospitality Relief Dashboard – an invaluable and free portal of support for the entire hospitality industry that included more than 700 resource links that to this day are still being updated. National chains down to local mom and pops relied on this single source of information to navigate through many topics, like how to get access to relief funds and the ever-changing case counts and governmental mandates.

Throughout my interviews, I heard similar stories of the many types of support needed to get through the early days.

2. CALCULATING THE BURN RATE

> *"It fundamentally alters the business right to the point where*
> *you move into survival mode. What is my cost of staying*
> *open and doing business? And how long can I survive?"*
> – John Cywinski, President of Applebee's

First came the financial concerns. After it was clear the pandemic would not soon be over, leaders needed to get a handle on how much cash was being burned. Whether it was a result of government mandates or individual fear that kept consumers from walking through the doors, the result was the same: for many in the hospitality industry, there was little to no revenue, while in some instances, the costs of operation remained near constant in the early days.

John Cywinski brought this to life for me: "One of the early outcomes of this was franchisees and corporations all went into survival mode once they realized, this is serious. Pre-Covid, casual dining businesses were maybe 13% off premise. The vast majority of the businesses being dine-in, and then the government says, close your dining rooms. You immediately know that more than challenges your business model. It fundamentally alters it right to the point where you move into survival mode. What is my cost of staying open and doing business? And how long can I survive?"

He shared that every entity he knew of went into this survival mode, and I heard this same message time and time again in my interviews. It would be irresponsible not to quantify the burn rate, yet leaders had to do so without knowing whether this was going to last for weeks or months. No one at that point in time was thinking it was going to last beyond a year, let alone two years.

It could be easy in hindsight to offer suggestions on how leaders could have responded differently in those early days and pick out examples of businesses that did well, but let's be clear: in the moment, consumer fear was high and confidence was low, not a recipe for a booming traffic recovery. Businesses needed to find their own path forward to get to the next stage from merely surviving to sustaining their businesses.

Giving up was not an option! Leaders pushed onward.

SUSTAIN.

1. SUSTAINING AND FEEDING PEOPLE

"And when the doors closed across the country, so did the places that provided the emotional nourishment for our souls."
– Barry McGowan, CEO, Fogo de Chão

Stepping back to the basics, one definition of the word 'sustain' provided by Merriam-Webster says: "to give support or relief to." [5] So how do we think of a business sustaining itself? Before we answer that, we must consider what makes a business a business. It's the combination of three key stakeholders working together in harmony to make a business survive and thrive.

So how did the industry sustain its "Business" during the pandemic? By feeding all of them — employees, customers, and communities. Yet, it goes much deeper than just nourishing bodies.

When restaurants were closed, it was like the heartbeat of the community just stopped overnight. There was no joy. Barry McGowan confided with me about his feelings in the early days of the pandemic and what it meant not only for his restaurant chain but for the industry as a whole. In what might have been one of the most poetic

---

[5] "Sustain," December 25, 2022. https://www.merriam-webster.com/dictionary/sustain.

and profound comparisons I heard from anyone, Barry likened his experience at a deserted Legacy West shopping center in Plano, Texas to a verse from the iconic Don McLean song, "American Pie."

Do you remember how still and quiet the streets were in March of 2020?

As he looked out on Legacy West, once filled with vibrancy and energy, only to have become eerily silent overnight, it felt like "the day the music died." Barry shared, "I'm literally standing in Legacy West – a vibrant retail trade area. Usually, it's alive, all the time buzzing. And literally at this moment, I'm standing out there looking around – completely quiet, no music. Everything is dark. Nobody walking around. It was the eeriest feeling of my life. That was a defining moment for me. And it's literally the song… the day the music died."

Restaurants and retail in every community create a vibe and social connectivity that we took for granted. Without restaurants and retail shops, our communities are soulless. He explained that the industry hires the young kids who need jobs or are just starting their careers. They bring the energy, the love of all the things we can define about the way we feel when we go out somewhere.

Barry recalled to me an interaction with a member of the local police department. The police officer saw Barry standing in the empty plaza just gazing at the emptiness. The patrol car pulled up and the officer rolled down his window to ask, "Are you OK?"

As a lifelong veteran of the industry, Barry simply replied what came naturally to him, "Are you hungry? Do you want some lunch?" He went on to tell that officer to make sure he went back and told all of his fellow officers that Fogo de Chão was still feeding people. For the coming days, weeks, and months, Barry and the Fogo family shifted gears to feeding the community. Barry closed that story with, "That's the point of our restaurant industry. If we're not feeding people, we can't help the community."

In the midst of all of this uncertainty, restaurants kept feeding people, anyone in need —employees, customers, first responders — not for commercial reasons, but because it's what the industry does even with little to no revenue coming in. However, it quickly became apparent that while the industry was functionally nourishing the body, we, as consumers, were missing something important – the emotional connections.

In an effort to flatten the curve, we unintentionally flattened our communities. The millions of hospitality frontline workers who were the heartbeat of our favorite activities were sent home. And when the doors closed across the country, so did the places that provided the emotional nourishment for our souls. With each day, month, and year that passed, it became clear that restaurants and the many other closed businesses were indeed 'essential' to our well-being.

There are countless examples of the restaurant industry feeding communities. I will share more in the coming chapters.

2. DATA, BUT NO INSIGHTS

Unfortunately, when businesses go into survival mode, the consumer's needs and wants are left behind more often than not. March of 2020 was no exception.

Throughout the early months, there was certainly data about the "virus" – what I call the "voice of the virus." Each and every day there was a flood of new information and new mandates that needed to be sorted. If you were a multi-unit operator in more than one town or state, you had to be aware of the rules of engagement, closures, and capacity constraints, which varied by state, by county, and even by city municipality. It was a tangled web of data that paralyzed policy makers with its complexity.

However, consumer insights were in short supply during those early days. The "voice of the customer," as we in the marketing research field call it, needed to be infused into the conversations in order to get out of survival mode into sustaining and growing businesses.

When it comes to consumer research, often there is a rush to get to *'the answer.'* You can't order a research project like you would order at a fast food drive-thru. It takes work knowing what the question is and the best way to get the answer we are seeking. Back in my early days at Frito-Lay, if stakeholders 'ordered' a research study without enough thought into the objectives and questions, we'd fondly ask our stakeholder, "Would you like fries with that focus group?"

Tackling the questions of Covid was no different. Within a few weeks, there was no lack of free consumer data available, all with good intentions, no doubt. Yet in the rush to get *the answers*, identifying the key questions was missed, in my humble opinion. When the question isn't clear, how can the answer be clear or insightful?

Barry recounted the reasons why my research stood out to him: "Lisa, yours was the first research that came out that actually did two things. First, it used the term 'joy,' which resonated with us, because that's what we talked to our team about." He continued, "Next, it wasn't about Covid – we had too much data on that. In fact, the graphs were conflicting. Everybody was asking questions, but nobody was asking consumers, 'How do you feel?' 'What do you want?' and 'What would make you feel normal?' So, your research really resonated with us immediately."

GROW.

1. WHEN EVERYTHING IS ON THE LINE AND THERE'S NOTHING TO LOSE

"Our ability to be nimble and flexible and agile was essential."
– John Cywinski

When everything's on the line, you figure out a way to get stuff done. Innovation is the lifeblood of brands keeping them relevant and staying current, but it can be a long, arduous process.

And when there is nothing to lose, it becomes easier to try anything and everything. That's exactly what happened. Businesses became scrappy; they pivoted to create solutions previously deemed impossible – not because they wanted to, but because they had to. The old adage "Innovate or die" rang true in businesses across the country.

One common thread across all my interviews was a company-wide commitment to innovation. Teams came together to generate ideas that rallied behind the industry's core value of serving customers and communities to create joy… and create much-needed revenue! Everybody had their own perspective on what was dragging their businesses down and what their top priorities were on the path to addressing those issues. Pride was put to the side during those times because it did not matter who came up with a winning idea, everyone in the organization stood to benefit if it worked. Innovation came in many different forms: virtual classes, pop-up parking lot dining areas, meat shops, phone applications. You name it, we saw it.

2. DEVELOPING A FRONTIER MINDSET

As a backdrop, it's no revelation that the full-service industry was suffering from somewhat of an identity crisis as consumers flocked to fast casual restaurants for high-quality food that was faster and cheaper than the casual dining experience. This was compounded by not having the drive-thru convenience of fast-food restaurants. Even prior to the start of the pandemic, many full-service restaurants were already suffering from declining traffic as a result of changing behaviors and preferences.

So, when there was no business to be had, management teams spent every waking minute laser-focused on innovating. Leaders quickly moved into what I like to call a "frontier mindset," which is what pushed the early Americans to get out of their comfort zones and head west in search of new opportunity. These Americans were the pioneers of their day – the risk-takers who decided the status quo was just not good enough. They were going to be the ones to push boundaries and see if there was something better in uncharted territory.

Modern-day business is no different, and the frontier pioneers of the hospitality and restaurant industries were the ones who helped keep doors open in preparation for when the pent-up demand from consumers would be unleashed.

It's not the "what they did," but more the "how they did it." Importantly, it's how to do it again and again. It was a remarkable acceleration of so many things. Yet, I would say it will all have been pointless and useless if those innovation principles aren't harnessed, so I created an entire chapter dedicated solely to innovation.

LESSONS LEARNED

As we navigated through the three early stages of Covid that Ricky Richardson called, 'Sustain. Survive. Grow', a few key insights emerged.

1. CLARITY OF PURPOSE AND CALLS TO ACTION DROVE SUCCESS

We found out how much we all had in common. Whether it was the restaurant owner, busser, food supplier, or the dine-in customer, everyone craved clarity. The human brain can withstand immense pressure under the right circumstances and having a vision for what is to come can help create that environment.

Uncertainty breeds anxiety and anxiety directly impacts behaviors both in the moment and in the future. Without the clarity many of the leaders possessed, it is safe to assume even more businesses would have remained closed.

2. WHEN WE WERE TOLD TO STAY HOME TO FLATTEN THE CURVE, WE FLATLINED OUR COMMUNITIES

As the doors closed across the country, so did the places that provided the emotional nourishment for our souls.

What's interesting is that when you talk about restaurants going back to basics, it typically means operations. It's the fundamentals of service, food, and value. I want to challenge that here. We learned during Covid that 'back to basics' is really about delivering joy, not just those functional elements. From the early days of feeding employees and communities, restaurants delivered not just food, but much-needed joy that revived struggling neighborhoods. In those moments, restaurants brought life, energy, and a human connection to communities that basically were otherwise dark.

3. RELENTLESS FOCUS ENABLED THE SPEED OF INNOVATION

There was a laser focus on not necessarily coming up with the best suggestions, but instead thinking of as many as possible. The fear of new ideas failing was tossed out the window early on when there were no clear solutions.

A brutal level of focus and willingness to try new initiatives allowed for the implementation of solutions we would have previously thought impossible. Ideas that would normally take months or years to develop, test, and execute happened in mere days – because there was no time or margin for delay.

A LITTLE TENSION RELIEF, PLEASE

In those early days, I probably wasn't the only one that went shopping for two weeks of groceries and cleaning supplies... and even buying an extra pack of toilet paper. At the peak of the early chaos, my husband, and maybe some of you, went so far as to pay outrageous prices for that liquid gold called hand sanitizer. How about $90 for two small bottles of hand sanitizer, more than it would have cost for a steak dinner! I'm not making this up, it happened!

Grocery shelves were blown out by March 14, 2020
Photo by Lisa W. Miller

THE BUSINESS OF JOY

> *"Joy comes to us in moments —*
> *ordinary moments. We risk missing*
> *out on joy when we get too busy*
> *chasing down the extraordinary."*
>
> – Brené Brown

Did you ever think joy could be taken for granted?

THAT PROBABLY SOUNDS absurd since most normal, healthy individuals want to be happy and avoid the things that threaten to make us otherwise. But as we live, or should I say lived before the pandemic, how much about the daily joyful experiences did we just assume were a given? In what felt like an instant, so many of the things that once brought us joy ceased to exist, sending a ripple through our communities. Restaurants, hotels, and other joy-based businesses were not struggling because the industry was slow in reacting to a change in consumer needs; the world around us had changed – quickly.

Since the pandemic, I have candidly become obsessed with spreading the message to focus on "joy, not fear" to get to the other side of that challenging season. Our research confirms the healing power of joy. Through these troubled times, we have seen a pervasive theme of gratitude, kindness, and courage as humans looked up from their devices and paused from their busy lives to appreciate the simple joys of caring for one another. From the healthcare workers on the front lines, to our closest friends and families, it's the human connections that make life worth living. While it was founded during the pandemic, my hope is that The Journey Back to Joy becomes a lasting movement.

But the early pandemic talk was no longer about joyful activities like making plans to go out or visit family. The talk mostly revolved around the number of cases, hospitalizations, people dying, and the need to stay home. There were entire social media movements dedicated to driving home how important it was to, well, *stay home.* At times it felt as if there was an entire culture of shaming anyone who thought of venturing outside. A common belief emerged that if you were not trying to solve the problem, you must be contributing to it. We are going to go deeper into this later, but for now it is important to realize that actions designed to make us feel safe and protect us, ended up scaring us, ultimately having unintended and negative consequences on the economic recovery.

THE CONSUMER PERSPECTIVE

1. GETTING BACK TO NORMAL?

When we reached the first plateau where the pandemic seemed to be behind us, the conversation changed to how we could get back out to our "regularly scheduled programming." We heard terms like the "new normal," which, candidly, I despised as it missed the point that consumer needs stayed the same, but how consumers accessed them is what really changed. Then we had a resurgence of cases and a return to lockdown, and that momentary joy was stripped again. This rollercoaster would not only make a return to normalcy difficult in the short term, but also hurt consumer confidence going forward. It would also continue to hurt consumers' engagement with each other as the divide between staying home or going out, mask or no mask, vaccine or no vaccine remained in the forefront of mainstream media and social media. It was the initial foreshadowing of some unruly behavior we would see more of as the pandemic unfolded.

The question during the pandemic was – when would the moment arrive that consumers would be ready to venture back out? While the world was paralyzed by the data and uncertainty of the virus, I was focusing on mapping the consumer re-entry.

There was a lot of free consumer data out there, but as I mentioned before, I firmly believed that they were asking the wrong questions. Standard research questions like, "On a five-point scale, how likely are you to visit a restaurant in the next 30 days?" were being used. The answers were being reported, but honestly, how could a consumer even answer that question when our knowledge and understanding of the virus literally changed daily? There had to be a better way to predict and anticipate the recovery.

2. BRINGING FORWARD THE VOICES OF THE CONSUMERS

Sharing the data is one thing, yet when you hear directly from consumers in their own words, their unfiltered comments highlight the raw emotions of the joy that was taken away when the world shut down. We wanted to understand what it was about these activities that was so special. Why did these activities give them so much joy?

Well, let's take a look at what some of the consumers we spoke to said when asked what brought them joy....

THE JOY OF BREAKING BREAD TOGETHER

"I like that feeling of being taken care of at restaurants when meals are made to your taste. Mostly, I truly enjoy traveling the world through food and experiencing other cultures through restaurants."

Breaking bread is something human beings have done throughout the ages to connect with others on a deeper level. From first dates to celebrating milestone events, food creates connection. It was not until we were told that our favorite places were now off-limits, or that our party size had to be under a certain number of guests that many of us realized just how much joy there was in the restaurant experience. While restaurants did their best to adapt with dine-at-home experiences and cocktails to-go, it never quite filled the need for socialization.

Again, I am in the consumer business. My clients are in the consumer business. We need to deliver an amazing customer experience or the people we serve do not need us. If we are in the coffee business and we don't wow the customer with both quality and hospitality, they will simply make their coffee at home and embrace the isolation. Thankfully, that is not the case for the clients with which I work – companies that recognize and deliver exceptional service always strive to make customers feel valued.

THE JOY OF LIVE CONCERTS

"Music is organic - people naturally respond to it, resonating in us like our own hearts beating. When it is shared with others it becomes a connector of the human experience. It helps my soul."

Live concerts bring joy because....
May 2020

"Music is organic - people naturally respond to, resonating in us like our own hearts beating. When it is shared with others it becomes a connector of the human experience. It helps my soul."

JourneyBackToJoy

The Joy of Live Concerts

It doesn't matter what genre of music you listen to. The size of the venue and number of people in attendance aren't crucial factors. Just being around other people who share the same excitement you do for the band or artists pouring their hearts and souls out on stage is exhilarating. It is almost impossible to put into words just how electrifying the energy can be; shoulder-to-shoulder singing along with strangers in a crowded dive bar or waving a cell phone light in the air with thousands of other raving fans. Even if concerts are something you only go to once or twice a year, they were sorely missed during the shutdowns.

THE JOY OF THE THEATER

"When the actor's performances are fantastic, I feel transported in time and part of the storyline. It makes me feel involved and totally immersed in another world for a much too short time without my normal worries and stresses."

This quote reinforces just how important it is to escape from reality, even if just for a short period of time, and the theater does that through personal connection. The actors and actresses are in the theater with us, not in a faraway land or on a recording where we can rewind or fast-forward at will. No, these are living breathing people giving every ounce of their creative selves for the benefit of those in attendance. For any lover of the arts, there was no trade-off for losing access to live performances. Even harder still was the effect on the performers, who had no option of taking their acts elsewhere and were forced to ride out the storm offstage.

THE JOY OF SHOPPING – RETAIL THERAPY

"Retail shopping in stores is very therapeutic for me. It's not only an opportunity to treat myself (or others), but it also provides me with the excitement and adrenaline rush I enjoy when I discover great deals, new or uniquely designed items for myself or loved ones."

May 2020
Shopping in stores brings joy because...

"Retail shopping in-stores is very therapeutic for me. It's not only an opportunity to treat myself (or others), it also provides me with the excitement and adrenalin rush I enjoy when I discover great deals, and new or uniquely designed items for myself or loved ones."

JourneyBackToJoy

The Joy of Shopping

Can joy from in-store retail shopping even be a thing? There are two opposite sides of this debate for sure: the people who think frivolous shopping is wasteful and those who make it an everyday activity. While they might have been at odds all the time prior to the pandemic, the loss of something many did not appreciate quickly became very serious, and it had nothing to do with the act of spending money. That was still possible through online retailers. What was missing was the human part of the experience, being around others while purchasing or window shopping. There was a community and subculture in retail shops that no delivery service could replace.

THE BUSINESS PERSPECTIVE

1. FINDING AND DELIVERING JOY IN UNEXPECTED WAYS

> *"Restaurants don't just feed us; they nourish our souls"*
> – Anita Adams, CEO, Black Bear Diner

Anita Adams, CEO of Black Bear Diner, shared a story that highlighted how restaurants brought joy to customers during the pandemic, regardless of the sometimes less-than-desirable circumstances. With dining rooms closed across their system, Black Bear Diner, like many other restaurants, created makeshift parking lot patios to offer a "dining-in" experience as best they could. Anita recalled a particularly funny, yet heartwarming story of a location in Reading, CA: "So we have a tent, and we have tables, but the patio slants towards the building. It's December, it's cold, and it's rainy. It's this undesirable setting, right, but it worked for our customers. This speaks to brand love they have for the Bear." The patio was not only full of happy customers, but it also brought energy and life back to the community.

She went on to say, "The dining experience has been validated as so much more than feeding the stomach. I never realized how much I enjoyed sitting at a bar in a restaurant having a glass of wine next to my husband with the buzz of talking and clanking of dishes until I was no longer able to do it."

She explained that customers would send them little notes about their love of the brand, plus some customers mentioned picking up food three times a week to help them "hang in there." No matter how long you have done something, there is always an opportunity to learn something new or see things from a different perspective.

As we discussed earlier, dining out feeds our souls. That is probably what hurt the most over the two-plus years of the pandemic – the raw, emotional element of having our souls starved. That is why the business of joy matters. Everyone was looking for some variation of the same thing, and the best thing any of us could do was to embrace and support that desire.

2.   THE BUSINESS OF JOY PAID OFF

> *"Our job in hospitality is to make sure we are creating an environment so the customers can have what they desire, not what we desire."*
> – **Barry McGowan**

I remember Barry McGowan saying that this research really inspired him because it was about what they *did* – the purpose of their job in hospitality was to deliver joy. It made such an impact on him that Fogo de Chão began calling its Covid blueprint "The Journey Back to Joy," which was grounded in this research and rooted around what it could give guests amid pandemic conditions instead of on what was stripped away. By October 2020, just six months after the pandemic started, Fogo de Chão had returned to 95% of 2019 sales, with 18 stores even posting increased sales, year-over-year. They accomplished this feat despite reduced capacities – more than 50% of restaurants in their system were limited to half their capacity.

"That shows you the thesis paid off," McGowan says. "People were going out. People wanted to go somewhere where they could just enjoy themselves and leave behind what was going on in the world, even for a short while."

Yet, many restaurant experiences were not so joyful. Barry continued to reflect that he was often disappointed when he dined out as a consumer, as several of his favorite restaurants eliminated items in the wake of the pandemic. Covid was used as an excuse to cut costs

— and in some cases, *corners* — where possible. Management made decisions for a number of reasons, although they seemingly did not consider what their customers would want.

People want to get back to normal and feel like they have control again, which is hard to do when you walk into your favorite restaurant and see that everything has changed because it served the bottom-line interest of the business, not the customer's interest. McGowan ended that thought by saying, "Our job in hospitality is to make sure we are creating an environment so the customers can have what they desire, not what we desire."

What a novel concept! But what does all of this really mean to the rest of us as we move forward?

MEASURING JOY AND THE ECONOMIC RECOVERY

After understanding what it meant for consumers to be without so many activities that brought them joy, my next goal was to create a path forward for businesses – a roadmap of sorts that could measure and predict the unleashing of the pent-up consumer demand. As I pondered the complexity of the problem, I drew back from my innovation days while working at Frito Lay. The model I sought to create had to paint a picture of a world that had never existed before. The recovery would be multidimensional and not found in a single answer to a single question, as many of the other surveys in those early days professed.

My hypothesis was that we had to map three key consumer dimensions in order to visualize and ultimately predict how the economic recovery would unfold:

1. Behaviors – what had consumers stopped doing or were doing less often?
2. Joy – what activities brought consumers the most joy?
3. Anticipation – what would consumers do first as they stepped back into activities outside their homes?

I fondly referred to this chart as the Journey Back to Joy Bubble Chart. So, in April 2020, my company, Lisa W. Miller & Associates, released a national research study asking 1,000 Americans who were 18 years of age and older what activities they could no longer participate in that used to provide them the most "joy." The number one answer by a landslide was dining out, with a whopping 81% response rate. When asked about the first activity people planned on doing again once they could, going to restaurants was the clear leader with an 86% response rate.

The visual below shows the intersection of these three key consumer dimensions – behaviors, joy, and anticipation as the doors of the activities we thought were getting ready to reopen again.

The Journey Back To Joy - MAY 2020

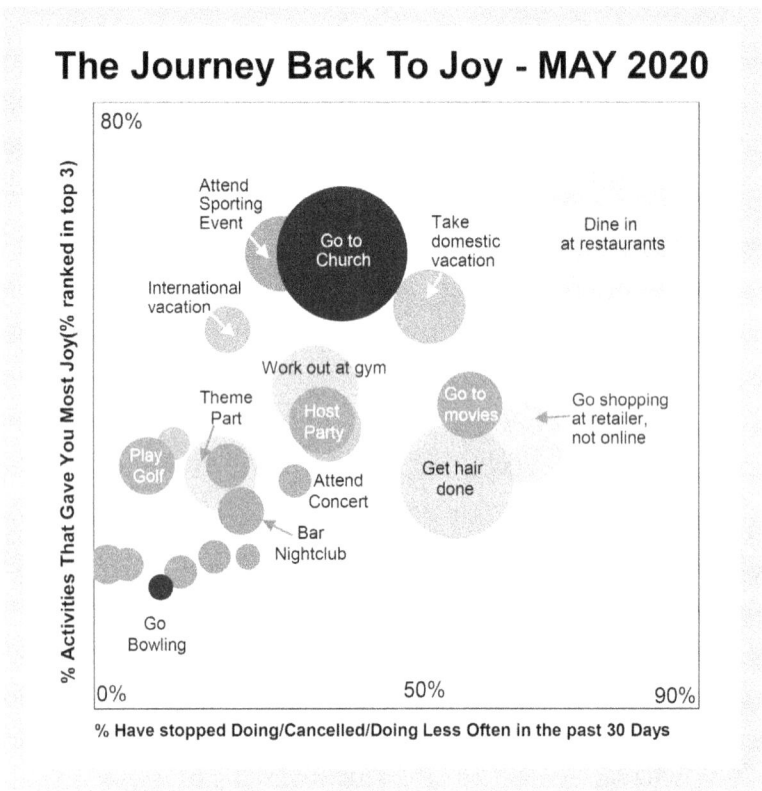

Bubble chart. Y-axis: % Activities That Gave You Most Joy(% ranked in top 3), ranging from 0% to 80%. X-axis: % Have stopped Doing/Cancelled/Doing Less Often in the past 30 Days, ranging from 0% to 90% (with 50% marked). Labeled activities: Attend Sporting Event, Go to Church, Take domestic vacation, Dine in at restaurants, International vacation, Work out at gym, Theme Part, Host Party, Go to movies, Go shopping at retailer, not online, Play Golf, Attend Concert, Get hair done, Bar Nightclub, Go Bowling.

1. Behaviors – what had consumers stopped doing or were doing less often? (The horizonal axis)
2. Joy – what activities brought consumers the most joy? (The vertical axis)
3. Anticipation – what would consumers do first as they stepped back into activities outside their homes? (The size of the bubble)

Let's dissect why each of these is important.

1. BEHAVIOR: MEASURING THE PENT-UP DEMAND

The first dimension, behaviors, was painfully obvious and straightforward – the measuring of the pent-up demand itself. In research terms, this foundational metric identified the percentage of people who reported they had stopped doing these normal activities or were doing them less often. This output became the horizontal axis of the chart. If we think of this as a literal map, the activities on the far right, the east side of the map, were the activities with the most pent-up demand. The activities on the left are ones fewer people participated in from a business perspective.

Which activities had the highest pent-up demand in the early days of the pandemic?

Not surprisingly, dining out and shopping were activities that were missed by the most consumers in those early days. One of the more curious activities that was also high on the list was getting our hair done (cut, color, etc.). There's something very personal about this. There is the functional side of getting a haircut or color, but there's also an emotional or confidence boost that also happens. We know that for many, that time in the chair is also a bit of an escape. Going to the movies and taking a vacation rounded out the high pent-up demand activities.

The top activities with the most pent-up demand in May of 2020 were:	
Dine in at restaurants	77%
Go shopping at retailer, not online	63%
Go to the movies	56%
Get hair done	54%
Take a domestic trip/vacation	50%

2. ANTICIPATION: WHAT CONSUMERS WILL DO FIRST

When consumers are fearful, choices get made regarding which activities would take priority over others – which activities would be leaders of the economic recovery versus which activities would be sidelined until later. Additionally, with the compounded financial pressures, those *experiences* would have to be "worth it" to venture out and "risk" the uncertainties of the virus. Remember, this was in the early days of the pandemic when information about how the virus was transmitted literally changed daily, if not hourly. The size of the bubble in the chart indicates what consumers told us they wanted to do first when the doors opened. The top five activities people were looking forward to doing first were:

The top five activities people were looking forward to doing first were:	
Going to church	67%
Dining out at restaurants	66%
Getting hair done	61%
Working out at a gym	49%
Going shopping at a retailer	45%

That's right, getting hair done was in the top five for both pent-up demand and the first activities people were looking forward to getting back to. Something so many of us might have just taken for granted. Yet, we discovered it was more sorely missed than anyone could have expected when it was taken away. Social media was flooded with tips and tricks about DIY hair care to fill the void of going to the local salon. This, of course, came with almost as many horror stories of DIY gone wrong, or images of men having shoulder-length hair, or those just letting the gray shine through. Hair stylists began offering home hair color kits. Vibrant hair colors — pinks, blues, greens, purples, and even silvers — skyrocketed on social media as consumers found joy as they worked or attended school from home by adding a bit of color to their hair.

Working out at the gym might not have made the list for pent-up demand, but interestingly enough, it was something people looked forward to doing when they could. Exercise falls under the category of self-care, but there is so much more to it. Home gyms and workout regimens might have been able to fill the functional void better than the hair care hacks, but it was the interpersonal aspect many longed to get back. Even if you are not speaking to the person on the treadmill next to you, there is an energy and sense of community that comes from working out with others.

3. JOY – PRIORITIZING THE JOY

Figuring out how to measure joy was a challenge. I didn't want to just ask about joy on a traditional five-point research scale; I wanted to understand what activities were most joyful because those would be the activities consumers were most connected to emotionally. Out of 30 activities, I asked consumers to tell me which were the top three activities that gave them the most joy. I believed these joyful activities would be the ones consumers craved the most, felt most empty when they were stripped away, and that would be prioritized as the doors reopened. I called this the Joy Axis. The activities that were further north on the map were the ones consumers found most joyful.

Below are the top five activities in which people found the most joy:	
Dine in at restaurants	*61%*
Attend professional or college sporting events	*60%*
Go to church	*60%*
Take a domestic trip/vacation	*53%*
Take an international trip/vacation	*50%*

One of the activities that stands out here is sports. Attending sports events is not quite as common an activity as going to the salon or gym, so it missed the lists for pent-up demand, but it made number two on the list for overall joy. The sporting world progressed through a series of changes just like other industries as those in charge tried to keep teams playing and fans watching. In the beginning, games were held without fans, and it just was not the same. Do you remember when sports soundtracks were added? It helped a bit. Some fans were even paying to have life-size cardboard replicas of themselves placed in the seats at events. How much would you pay to have your cardboard likeness perfectly placed to be seen during the prime-time coverage of the 2021 Super Bowl football game? Can you imagine how that conversation must have gone when the National Football League was brainstorming that idea and how much to charge? The NFL decided to sell 30,000 cutouts for $100 each to fill in empty seats raking in a cool $3 million.[6] That's innovation at its finest. That $3 million is higher than the annual volume of many individual restaurants!

Church is another activity many might not expect to see rank so high on this list. Prayer is not something one needs to do in a group setting. In fact, it is often considered to be a solemn and solitary activity. Much like sports, religious events for almost any denomination could be

---

[6] Gaines, Cork. "The Super Bowl Will Have 30,000 Cardboard Fans to Help the Game Look Full and Keep Real Fans Socially Distant." Insider, February 7, 2021. https://www.insider.com/super-bowl-cardboard-fans-capacity-covid-2021-2.

watched on television, but the experience was not the same. The sense of community from worshiping as a group had been lost. As worshiping inside churches and synagogues was taken away, Google searches for prayer surged. *The Telegraph* reported, "In March 2020, the share of Google searches for prayer surged to the highest level ever recorded, surpassing all other major events that otherwise call for prayer, such as Christmas, Easter and Ramadan, analysis has revealed."[7] Whether it be as a fan in the audience cheering for your favorite team or a congregant in the pews singing hymns, both of these activities transcend functional experiences. They provide emotional and spiritual engagement.

LESSONS LEARNED

1. NEW CHALLENGES REQUIRED NEW TOOLS

During these uncertain and stressful times, it became apparent things were changing. I am not a big fan of the word "things" but considering how all-encompassing this change was, it might be the only word to do it justice. How we spoke was different. Our expectations about safety and customer service became jaded. The way we felt about our fellow human beings and the choices they made morphed into a polarizing landscape of fear and divisiveness. But on top of all this, it was the way we measured demand that needed to undergo the most significant change.

Measuring pent-up demand was a relatively new concept in the market research world since we had not witnessed another period in our lifetimes when so much was taken away so quickly. A framework had to be created to theorize and ultimately predict what would happen when the bubbling demand was finally unleashed. Our data proved that the economic recovery happened not by measuring one dimension, but by the intersection of three measures: behaviors, joy, and anticipation.

---

[7] Kelly-Linden, Jordan. "Pandemic Prompts Surge in Interest in Prayer, Google Data Show." The Telegraph, May 22, 2020. https://www.telegraph.co.uk/global-health/climate-and-people/pandemic-prompts-surge-interest-prayer-google-data-show/.

2. ASKING THE RIGHT QUESTIONS

In the world of marketing research, it seems today there is always a rush to find "the" answer without really thinking about the question itself. We learned during the pandemic that it's important to draw upon past experiences, yet old tools and old questions just wouldn't have worked. As research professionals, we were forced to change the way we did our job, much like everyone else had to change.

Think about it like using a map. While it's nice to see how far we've traveled, it's more important to know how to get to where we are going. Asking the right question creates the map to get to the insights. The right questions become forward-looking and can illuminate the road ahead instead of keeping you glued to the rearview mirror. When you have well-articulated questions combined with analytical skills, that's when the magic happens.

3. SUSTAINED DEPRIVATION FROM JOY CHANGED US

Seeking joy is not new because of the pandemic. Joy is a fundamental human need. It is not a fad or trend; it is something we all need every day of our lives. It sustains and energizes us. It gets us through tough times. Yet, during the months and years leading up to Covid, it was like we had all gone on autopilot. We've painted the picture here to show just how integral restaurants and other activities are in providing joy. Even the word 'restaurant' itself comes from a French word meaning 'to restore or refresh.' We all were forced to pause during Covid, and it reminded us that joy and restoration are important.

I think most would agree that human beings are good at heart and want to co-exist peacefully. Whenever we encounter challenging events like natural disasters, tragedies in the community, or famine in other parts of the world, the spirit of generosity kicks in and we all pitch in to help one another. When the world paused in the early days of the pandemic, this very human kindness and empathy were on full display. There was great concern about keeping each other safe - especially those in the highest risk categories - and doing what we were told was necessary to stop the spread. But as the lockdown wore on and it became apparent that things were going to drag on for some time, those sentiments slowly started to change.

4. FORESHADOWING OF THE BAD CUSTOMER BEHAVIOR TO COME

When we are told we can't do something, it makes us want to do it more. It lights a fire of appreciation for the things that bring us joy while also opening us up to new choices we might not otherwise have considered. These truths have been the catalyst and needed spark for the economic recovery ever since government restrictions and mandates were lifted. What was noticed when the doors began opening, though, was that some of the kindness had evaporated. Expectations were high and patience was low – a recipe for tension and discomfort.

Like a prisoner in solitary confinement, our minds began to play tricks on us. We started out thinking everything would be OK if we just kept our heads down and did the time, but the continued uncertainty let doubt creep in. With each passing day we became more impatient. Many were venturing out in whatever capacity was allowed (and some that weren't) with high expectations. Whether it be the gas station, supermarket, or food service establishment, people expected the world, even though most of the world was still shut down. This became a recipe for disaster and foreshadowed the tension and discomfort that would ultimately unfold in the coming months.

None of this helped anyone. I've said it before and will say it again: joy, not fear, was the only path forward. And measuring joy still isn't over…

THE LANGUAGE
OF COVID

"It was a time of fear, and it was pretty intense. The reality of it was that with all the changes coming down from the government on a regular basis, consumers were confused and began immediately equating Covid with death."

– Jack Gibbons, CEO, FB Society Restaurant Brands

I N MARCH OF 2020, as the world faced an invisible threat and enemy, there were suddenly new, unfamiliar words and phrases forced upon us.

Quarantine. Isolation. Lockdown. Am I the only one who had to Google what "shelter in place" meant? Instead of being united against a common enemy, the new coronavirus, this language propelled us to become more divided, albeit with well-intended differences in beliefs about closures, masking, and vaccines. The science, which is typically clear and definitive, was suddenly blurry, uncertain, and unsettling.

As every day became quieter and more still, the language of Covid began to negatively impact our psyche. Amid all of this, business owners everywhere were struggling to sort through this new language to balance a responsible approach in which both physical and financial health were preserved.

1. IT'S NOT WHAT YOU SAY, BUT HOW YOU SAY IT

Taking a step back, we know that throughout history, words have been used to rally people behind, or against, countless causes. The persuasiveness of those speaking created the overall sentiment at that moment in time and helped solidify the outcomes. Speech, or any type of communication for that matter, is the lynchpin for how we relate to one another. Whether you believe it or not, words have power. Words can cut like a knife or mend a broken heart; however, it is not the words alone that create the impact. I grew up with the mantra "It's not what you say, but how you say it." There is something to be said for a charismatic way of delivering bad or unwelcome news. In medicine, it is referred to as bedside manner. How messages are conveyed can make or break how communication itself is received and the actions that follow.

In consumers' most recent memory prior to Covid, September 11, 2001 is probably the last time we saw words carry as much weight as they did during the pandemic. Leaders were very calculated and measured in the messages they were sending, and the words chosen to ensure the average American felt safe and hopeful. In those early days after September 11, we were urged to embrace our fellow citizens and continue living our lives without fear of going out to public places and taking part in joyful activities. There were so many negative, fear-inducing words that could have been used, given the magnitude of what had just happened, but instead the choice was made for positivity and unity.

Amid the initial fear of 9/11, pundits predicted that Americans would be fearful of flying. At the time, it was widely believed many would never get on an airplane again because the fear outweighed the joy. That didn't happen. Over time, people got back to focusing on *living* instead of being fearful. Though the travel experience did change drastically from what it was before the attack, with time, we still moved forward.

A LITTLE TENSION RELIEF, PLEASE
Some of the new language also made us laugh.

It would be remiss of me not to touch on the incredible and sometimes jumbled language that made us laugh during the early days of Covid. It is actually hard to trace back where these words actually started but they did lighten the mood through all the terrifying language. Does anyone remember Quarantini, Zoombombing, or Blursday? Even in the worst of times, Americans didn't disappoint in trying to make light of a serious situation. We all needed a bit of joy and laughter in those early days. There were countless examples out there, but below is a list of some of my favorites.

Blursday – no one knew what day it was because it all blurred together

Quarantini – cocktail consumption while in isolation

Covidiot – someone who ignores public health advice

'Rona – because we have to shorten everything

Maskne – acne breakouts from wearing facial masks

Covexit – strategy of when we will exit lockdown

Zoombombing - like photobombing when unexpected things pop into your zoom meet

Doomscrolling – quickly reading the fear inducing headlines on your phone

Covideo party - online parties

LWM

2. "WARTIME" LANGUAGE DURING "PEACETIME"

While the goal here is not to compare the Covid pandemic to the vicious attacks on our nation, it is important to see the similarities in how words were used. For almost two years and two administrations, from the very first moment when businesses began to close down, we heard around the world wartime words like: *isolation, quarantine, lockdown,* and many others that evoked or instilled a sense of fear and despair among a significant number of Americans, as shown by our data. The community and people around us began to look like a threat to our personal health and safety, and many acted accordingly. Even parents reported in our data that many children were anxious and asking about the virus.

In a physical war, you have a clearly defined enemy. Everyone on your side knows where they are and can identify them by sight if need be. Looking out across the battlefield at an opposing army with their weaponry pointing back at you, there is no question of being killed if you did not kill them first. The government and the media rallied behind this same approach when it came to the invisible enemy of Covid, and they inundated us with all kinds of statistics to drive their point home. But because there was no known way to eradicate the virus, we wound up turning on each other and developed a greater distrust of the media and government.

The media reported nightly on various *shortages* in basic supplies, the rising number of cases and *deaths,* and *even the shortages of ventilators and hospital beds.* Regardless of how bad things actually were, the words and images used always seemed to amplify the messages, making everything feel worse.

The lingering fear of Covid is real and it is negatively impacting the economy. In October 2022, after two and a half years of the pandemic, over one third of Americans (36%) believed that Covid had permanently changed them into a more anxious person. The lockdowns and constant inundation of the Covid buzzwords and phrases have had a negative psychological impact for many. Only 45% of Americans report having fully returned to their normal frequency of activities.

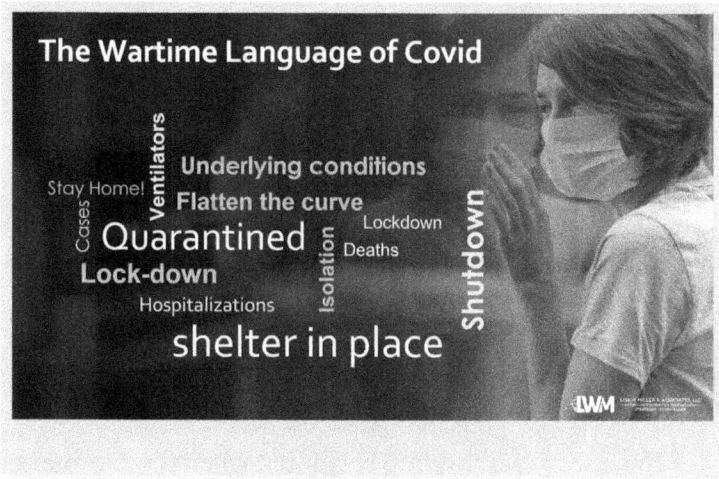

3. VACCINE CASE STUDY

> *"I am concerned about the unknown, long-term effects of the Covid vaccine."*
> – Consumer Verbatim, Summer 2021

A case in point is the language used to encourage people to get vaccinated. Reminder: I am "Switzerland" in this discussion, as an insights professional concerned with "how" and "what" happened during the pandemic; my concern is not what was right or wrong, too extreme, or not extreme enough. I will be looking at this topic through the lens of the consumer and the economic recovery and not any statement on public policy or the vaccine's efficacy – good or bad.

We began measuring consumer sentiment on vaccines back in April of 2020, as soon as the news of a possible Covid vaccine being ready by year's end hit the newswires and consumers' radar. At the time, the questions on business leaders' minds were:

- How many Americans would raise their hands and roll up their sleeves to get vaccinated?

- How would consumers feel about accelerated approvals in the wake of mounting cases and deaths?
- Would the vaccine provide the proverbial shot in the arm to jumpstart the economy as consumers became vaccinated?

We know how the initial rollout unfolded, but back then businesses were hopeful the vaccine might stimulate the economy. Let me hit a few highlights of the timeline:

APRIL 2020: Enthusiasm and excitement for the vaccine were high

- There was a resounding belief that when the vaccine became available, it would give consumers confidence, making them feel more comfortable resuming their activities. Not surprisingly, the data showed that consumers would have been more comfortable if the vaccine had been thoroughly tested, yet there was general acceptance of an accelerated vaccine. We asked consumers how important being vaccinated factored in their decision and in the comfort to venture out to activities.

> *Extremely/Very Important in returning to normal activities:*
>
> - *74%: Once a vaccine is thoroughly tested*
> - *63%: Once a vaccine is made widely available, even if traditional testing has not been completed*

SEPT 2020: Confidence waned as traditional testing proved unlikely

- The positive sentiment dramatically shifted away from a vaccine that would not have had the time for traditional testing to be completed. This was the first early warning indicator of what was to come, and that vaccine hesitancy would be more than expected.

> • *72%: Once a vaccine is thoroughly tested (down 2pt)*
>
> • *49%: Once a vaccine is made widely available, even if traditional testing has not been completed (down 14pt)*
>
> • *Only 22% of Americans reported wanting to get vaccinated as soon as the vaccine was made available*

DEC 2020: FDA announces Emergency Use Authorization for Covid-19 vaccines for people over 16 years of age

- Broadcasted on national television, the first Covid-19 vaccine was administered to a critical care nurse from New York City.

JAN 2021: As the vaccine became more widely available, many Americans sat on the sidelines

- "Vaccine hesitancy" wasn't a phrase widely used before the pandemic, but quickly became part of the language of Covid. Four in 10 consumers were on the fence, waiting, or undecided to take the vaccine. Our data below aligned with other data sources at the time. Those who said they would never take the vaccine consistently hovered around 15%.

> *Covid-19 vaccines are in development. Will you want to take the vaccine as soon as it becomes available to the public?*
>
> • *45% (114 million) Yes, I will take as soon as possible*
>
> • *40% (101 million) No, but I will wait or are not sure/ undecided*
>
> • *15% (38 million) No, not interested in ever taking it*

Would the fear of <u>not</u> taking the vaccine win over the fear of taking the vaccine?

As the vaccine was rolled out and the take-rate was less than stellar, there was a plethora of ads trying to persuade Americans to get vaccinated. For the 40% who were fence-sitters, what would persuade them to take the vaccine, considering many were fearful of the vaccine itself? Would the fear of <u>not</u> taking the vaccine win over the fear of taking the vaccine? Putting my marketing hat on, it's a messaging quandary.

Historically, many Public Service Announcements (PSAs) made their case by tapping into our fear of negative outcomes – two that still stand out to me were about drug usage: "Scared Straight" and "This is your brain on drugs." If these don't sound familiar, do a search to check them out.

There was a string of different television commercial approaches to introduce and encourage Americans to get vaccinated – with some commercials focusing on fear while some focused on joy.

- **Fear of personally dying.** Heart-wrenching stories of an unvaccinated loved one who on their deathbed wished they had been vaccinated.
- **Do it for them.** Stories of children encouraging their parents to get vaccinated so they wouldn't die and leave their children parentless.
- **Take the shot to get back to living.** These commercials prioritized joy over fear and reminded consumers about returning to their normal activities.

The commercials even pulled out the big names with past presidents, doctors, and celebrities all encouraging people to get vaccinated.

4. THE VACCINE LAUNCH DIDN'T JUMPSTART THE ECONOMY AS HOPED

For those who did take the vaccine early on, consumers did feel more "comfortable" returning to some normal activities, but it wasn't the unleashing of the pent-up demand that was expected. Like most other issues during Covid, the data was polarized. There were other forces at play that helped the 2021 Q2 economic boom. We will discuss those forces in the next chapter.

Now that you have taken the vaccine, which best describes how it has impacted you going back to your normal activities and routines, including the things you have stopped doing or have been doing less often? (April 2021)	
Immediately start doing all activities and routines again	*15%*
Gradually start doing most activities, but not all	*37%*
Will pick a few activities to start doing again or more often	*31%*
Will not add any activities back yet and will wait until things settle down more	*17%*

While I don't have specific advertising research on the vaccine television commercials — and boy, I wish I did — I can tell you that from my data those who were already anxious about the virus were also anxious about getting the shot, which on the surface might seem counterintuitive. But it's really not when you think about it. Uncertainty is a powerful feeling and one of the leading causes of fear in any situation. So, our data suggests that advertising to them through a fear message likely would make them more fearful not less so.

Our data does show that among the 31% who had not been vaccinated as of January 2022, just over a third reported that the pressure to get vaccinated makes them less likely to get it. Not surprisingly, the top reason is that it should be a choice, not a mandate. Other top reasons revolve around the thorough vaccine testing and lack of transparency about the risks.

Sure, there are those who don't ever want to get vaccinated, but a large group just wanted to know more about it. Think about it like shopping in the supermarket. Some shoppers don't need to see anything other than a brand name before tossing an item into their cart, others will read the claims touted on the front of the package as truth, and some like to turn the package over to read the full ingredient list and nutritional content before deciding. The same held true for the vaccine.

Because the vaccine was being used under FDA's Emergency Use Authorization, the manufacturers of the vaccine were not allowed to advertise the vaccine; only the government was. As a result, the typical risks that come with medicines were not included in the advertising, which might have precluded the decision to take the vaccine by those who simply wanted more information about the risks.

You mentioned that you haven't taken the vaccine yet. Which of the following are reasons that contribute to why you have not gotten vaccinated? (January 2022)	
I think it should be a personal choice, not mandated	57%
With vaccinated people still getting Covid, I don't think it works	49%
Long-term side effects	45%
I don't think the government is being transparent with all the details of the risks	45%
The testing was rushed	38%
All the pressure to get vaccinated makes me even less likely to want to get it	36%

5. NEWS MEDIA/ SOCIAL MEDIA BECAME PART OF THE PROBLEM

"The news has instilled fear in me."
– Female Boomer

The fear of the unknown was bad enough, but the fear of changing paradigms and uncertainty made us even more anxious. Every day was different. From how long the virus could survive on surfaces to homemade hacks to keep you safe, the conflicting narratives were endless. YouTube videos about leaving packaged goods in the garage for a day or two or wiping them down with antibacterial agents before putting them away went viral. I know I did both of these things for a few weeks before giving up on them.

People flocked to the internet in search of "helpful" information but instead were often met with disinformation or theories proving to be anything but useful. This caused outrageous behaviors in people who did things they normally never would have dreamed of. As a result, we wound up with a nationwide toilet paper shortage. What did toilet paper have to do with a virus? I still can't answer that question but will admit I was guilty of buying an extra pack of the white stuff from time to time.

As cases rose, so did anxiety and fear – not just about contracting the virus but also from an economic standpoint. The media reports bounced back and forth between the number of physical deaths and grim employment metrics reflecting all of the people out of work due to the shuttering of businesses. There was very little joy to be found anywhere and it felt like only numbers reported as "less terrible" than expected were celebrated.

6. BRAND MESSAGING – A SEA OF SAMENESS

Advertisers and marketers who were known for creative prowess and a way with words struggled to craft a message of unity a frightened public could embrace. Early pandemic commercials became lost in a sea of sameness. Gone were the unique advertisements for bustling eateries, rowdy sporting events, or intimate social gatherings – all of which used to evoke joy and prompt people to frequent these types of events.

Some companies gave up on advertising altogether, while those who did advertise seemed to be one and the same. Commercials opened up on somber music or slow piano music showing eerily similar images of desolate streets, sports venues, and shopping malls. They repeated phrases of "We're here for you," and "We will get through this together." At the end of the commercials, the music increased in pace as we saw people clapping, and cheering. All were well-meaning but missed the mark in a sea of sameness where joy had been stripped away.

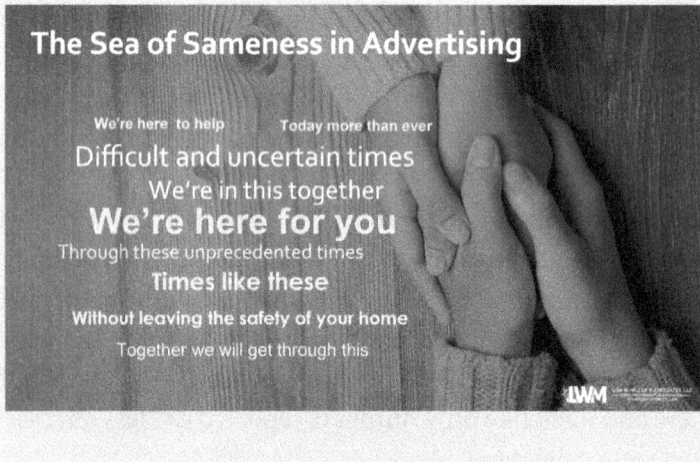

The lone bright spot in this advertising debacle was the opportunity it afforded the smaller, oftentimes more regional businesses to secure media time they might not have been able to get or afford before. Many national advertisers were pulling back on spending, causing massive advertising revenue declines because of the uncertainty surrounding the economy or simply because their doors were not open and the effort of bringing people to them would be futile. This became a win-win for both the television stations that were able to continue generating at least some revenue and the smaller businesses that were struggling to find ways of surviving or letting their clients know they were still open.

LESSONS LEARNED

1. WE BECAME SCARED OF EACH OTHER

While we were being bombarded with this new language of Covid, we lost our physical and emotional connections as well.

- Hugs and handshakes turned into elbow bumps.
- Smiles were covered by masks.
- Gathering with friends and family moved online or vanished altogether.

Jack Gibbons, the CEO of FB Society, echoed the familiar sentiment with me of just how scared we all suddenly became of one another. "It was a time of fear, and it was pretty intense. The reality of it was that with all the changes coming down from the government on a regular basis, consumers were confused and began immediately equating Covid with death. Nobody wanted to get it and give it to their loved ones. We all became scared of each other."

Mike Archer, CEO of Lou Malnati's Pizzeria, had his own take on the fear that had seemingly taken a hold on the world. "Employees were scared and concerned. What does social distancing even look like in a restaurant kitchen? Everything we dealt with was through the lens of how we keep our employees safe. There was this notion that grocery and health care workers were the main focal point of the essential worker conversations, yet restaurant workers also felt they were taking risks by going to work. Unfortunately, our employees weren't really perceived as being in that essential worker category by the public."

The pervasiveness of the fear during the pandemic was surreal but also very real, negatively impacting the economic recovery

2. NEW INDUSTRY LANGUAGE – "BE PREPARED TO BE CLOSED"

Industry leaders shared with me just how widespread the effects of this language of Covid were not just from the government mandates, but also in their own internal communications. From customers to employees, to first responders, to family members, everyone internalized the messages differently. Leaders had to be careful of how they translated initiatives or directives to their teams so as not to cause undue anxiety or stress. Any of those buzzwords we mentioned earlier in the chapter could have meant something different to each person on the team.

Margo Manning, former COO of Dave & Busters, shared with me how she had to find the measured words to convey a completely foreign concept. "Be prepared to be closed" with no time horizons for reopening. The conditions and mandates were already erratic enough, but the thought of waking up every morning and not knowing whether you would be able to open the doors or not made it incredibly difficult for leaders to plan.

When the doors closed for the first time at the start of the pandemic, everyone was in the same state of shock and not thinking beyond getting them open again. There was a collective sigh of relief when restrictions were lifted and leaders could get people back to work, but then the rollercoaster began. All of this had to be communicated to employees in the most empathetic of ways because their livelihoods were on the line.

This phrase might still be one of the most memorable statements of all my interviews – businesses had to "be prepared to be closed."

3. WHAT COULD HAVE BEEN DONE DIFFERENTLY?

That is always a difficult question since hindsight is 20/20, but joy was a common theme, even when it was because joy was missing, through the pandemic. Thinking back to the September 11th messaging where all of the messaging was positive, we could have led with an embrace of joyful activities while also focusing on safety and precautionary measures. This goes for everyone – from the local diner on the corner in your small town to all levels of government. Leading with joy can often lead to a positive result more so than instilling fear. Yes, fear may accomplish short-term behavior changes, but as all parents can attest to, it will not work in the long run and often spawns many unintended consequences – something about which we will go into more detail later on.

Much of the messaging that was designed to protect us wound up causing more harm than good. The constant use of negative words and phrases that made us immediately think about the virus led to fear and anxiety. It went further than just our individual existences as well, the language serving to polarize the nation as the months waned and no cure was in sight. And while we can learn from all of these things, it is also crucial to remember how we were at times able to still find joy during these times.

Masks were turned into fashion statements, goofy videos were made to encourage vaccinations, and we taught ourselves how to do a variety of different things at home we might not have tried otherwise. These homemade hacks were responsible for being the moments of light in a world of darkness.

Using wartime language created an 'enemy' to fight, but it unintentionally created an 'us vs. them' mentality. We are still paying the price for much of this language and behavior today even as restrictions are at all-time minimums and confidence has increased considerably. This matters more than many might realize. Words matter; how we market and communicate matters. We unintentionally made Covid the enemy from within and gave it the opportunity to tear us apart. We lost our connection with each other somewhere along the way. If we ever find ourselves in a similar situation again, we must remember that the economy cannot survive in an environment where everyone is scared to leave their homes. As with all things in life, balance is the key to surviving when times are rough and thriving when conditions are optimal.

4. WHAT WAS NOT BEING SAID

These actions by the media, and at a larger level by the government, led to a massive amount of distrust in many groups, and consumers were no different. In the beginning, most consumers had full faith in the data coming through the media from lawmakers and scientists. But as time went on, cases grew, and the pandemic evolved, that trust started to erode. Those who still trusted the experts became more fearful and it took longer for them to get back out. The declining trust led to a slower recovery, and we have seen tangible evidence that communities hit with the strictest lockdowns were the slowest to recover. What was designed to protect us wound up scaring us and causing long-term damage.

The fear and uncertainty, fueled by a new language of Covid, mesmerized and paralyzed at the same time, drawing us like moths to a flame. Looking back now, it is easier to see the similarities to wartime language. So, how would we expect this to play out in the hospitality industry? The common belief was that consumers would come out in droves once restrictions were lifted, but that was really not the case at all. Many were and still have been slow to return to the places where they once found joy.

THE TENSION BETWEEN FEAR AND JOY

"Mostly, we live in fear. That fear is manifested as our everyday anxieties where we find ourselves living in the regret of the past or grasping at the future. Joy is manifested in presence – that point at which we shed the past, let go of the future and are just there, where we are, in that moment."

– Michael J. Formica, EdM, NCC, LPC

F EAR MIGHT ARGUABLY be one of the most powerful emotions a human being can experience. From the fear of the dark to fear of others' beliefs, fear has a way of making people act in ways they normally would not. It is also fair to say, based on the data, that the pandemic pushed the needle for many Americans to a new breaking point of fear.

Maybe you were one of the people rocking back and forth, just waiting for the green light from government officials to open the doors to get back to your regular routine. Possibly you swore that you would wait it out until the virus was under control and had all but been eradicated. While those polar opposites existed, chances are you fell somewhere in the middle, having conversations with yourself and among family and friends about how you were feeling and what the right thing to do would be.

All of these conversations and thoughts running through people's minds about whether they wanted to venture out or not typically came while still in the safe comfort and confines of their own homes during the first six weeks of lockdown. The more time went by, the more our excitement to venture outgrew. Then, an unpredictable paradigm shift happened.

Do you remember how you felt in those early days?
Do you remember how hearing someone cough or sneeze within 20 feet of us caused a knee-jerk reaction to cross the street, give them a side-eye, or silently chastise them for being out in public? If yes, you weren't alone. By March 24, 2020, 74% agreed/strongly agreed with the statement "When I go out, I worry about the people that haven't been social distancing that I may be exposed to."

---

1. THEORY OF REOPENING COLLIDED WITH REALITY

When businesses finally began to reopen in May 2020, consumers didn't walk through the doors as expected. Most stayed home instead.

What happened?

Fear was greater than joy. Consumers paused and reflected: While the risk of personally getting sick in the pursuit of joy may have come with one set of stakes, the thought of getting a friend or loved one sick brought fear that often outweighed the benefits of the joy of venturing out.

People would generally agree that joy and fear are polar opposites, and they are. Yet, from a consumer standpoint, we must comprehend how they're similar despite their being on opposite sides of a behavioral continuum. Think of it like a tug-of-war rope that drove the economic recovery: when it comes to joy, it is what pulls us forward to venture out, and when we're afraid and fearful, it pulls us back and we stay home.

After six weeks of lockdown, consumers were pulling towards joy and the idea of venturing out again. The first states announced the doors would be reopening May 1st with 25% capacity. Consumers thought they were ready, but they weren't. Their readiness to venture out into the economy fell dramatically the week before the doors were reopened; that was the week of April 27, 2020. We saw this same pattern time and time again, state by state, as reopenings happened across the country. As the reopening dates grew closer, anticipation and excitement about venturing out grew, then boom! The week before reopening, fear again ruled the day. This fear was crippling to us as humans but also crippling for the U.S. economy.

By July 2020, the words *warfare, lockdown, shutdowns, isolations,* and *quarantine,* along with those frighteningly ominous phrases discussed in the last chapter, had taken their toll. Fear and anxiety peaked, with 50% of Americans being anxious or very anxious about stepping outside their homes to get back to normal activities.

From that point on and for the next two years, the ups and downs of the economic recovery were largely driven by the tug of war between joy and fear.

When the restaurant doors reopened, customers were still fearful.
Dallas Restaurant May 2020 - Photo by Lisa W. Miller

2. RE-ENTRY WAS A MINDSET, NOT A DEMOGRAPHIC

"Joy can be what pushes back against fear; fear can dissolve joy."
– Ira Rabois

Do you remember the images of Spring Break of 2020? Crowded beaches of college students partied like there was no pandemic. Those images, for better or worse, set the stage that younger Americans would be first out the door to spark and lead the economic recovery, and older consumers were going to stay home.

Well, that didn't happen either.

My thesis from the very beginning was that the economic recovery would look more like an innovation curve, not based on an age cohort or demographic group. The innovation curve is a pretty standard construct to how trial of new goods and service moves through our society. On the far left of an innovation curve, we have the innovators.

These are the absolute first to try new things as soon as they hit the market. It's a small group, but these people influence the rest of us. We all know someone who has to be the first to have the new technology or try the new restaurant that just opened. It's just in their DNA. Maybe you are the innovator in your group. The innovators in my thinking would be the first to venture out during Covid. As the model progresses through adoption, on the far right are the laggards. Those are typically the holdouts for whatever reason and the last to try new things or, during Covid, the last to venture outside.

Corporate America often invests in a particular type of research called a segmentation study. Literally and figuratively, we analyze the data to segment consumers, not based on demographics, but more their attitudes and behaviors. Why? The reason is that by identifying the segments, companies can target those who will find their offering most appealing, thus yielding the best return on investment. That is why I began conducting my consumer surveys, and to test my theory about mindset being a bigger indicator than demographics regarding who would come out first.

Think about your own friend groups or even people within your household. Were you all on the same page about when it would be safe to start venturing back outside? Maybe or maybe not. This really caused issues for a lot of people, with wide ranging debates on how safe or responsible it was to go back outside. Some people were so extreme in their feelings that they would stop speaking to extended family members. We saw the videos that went viral of people verbally attacking others on the street for not wearing a mask or standing too close to them – shocking behavior that foreshadowed things to come and how divided we became.

But think again about the people in your network. Maybe there is a boomer — somebody in their 50s or even 60s — who was just ready to get out the door as soon as possible and not really concerned about what was going on. On the other side, there were younger consumers who were anxious and still are to this very day. Whether someone admits it outwardly or not, we see signs of this everywhere. From younger consumers still wearing a mask because it was such a key part of their lives for so long to people who are still asking about vaccination status.

While we did say by and large that demographics were not an accurate indicator compared to psychographics, there was a very real gender divide regarding who was ready to get out in the world and who wasn't. Females tended to be much more anxious throughout the pandemic, which continued into the reopening phase. This had a ripple effect on the economy and reopening process as well, since many women are the decision makers in their households. If they are uncomfortable going out, you better believe they are not letting others under their roof go out, and many industries felt the brunt of that while brands with more of a male skew had better results in the beginning.

3. LET'S MEET THE RE-ENTRY SEGMENTS

One of the fun parts about doing marketing research segmentation studies is being able to answer the questions for yourself and see what segment you fit into. So, as I describe these segments, think about how you would have answered the questions back in March of 2020.

Ready?

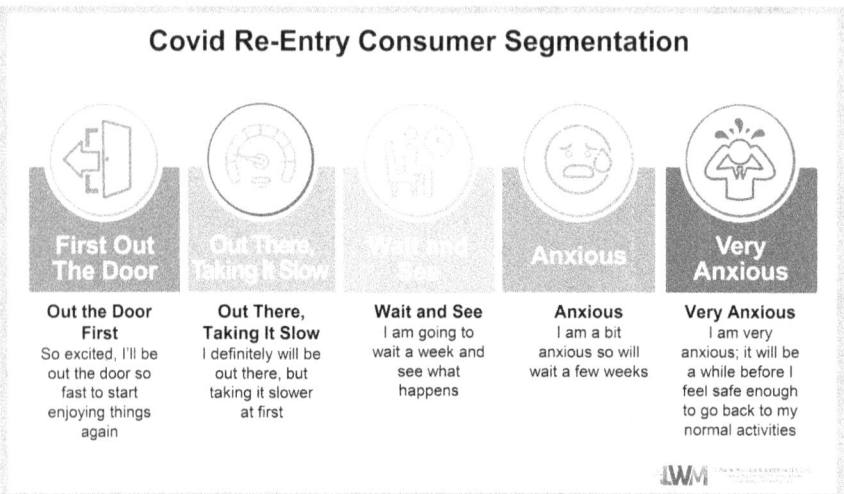

Covid Re-Entry Consumer Segmentation

First Out The Door	Out There, Taking It Slow	Wait and See	Anxious	Very Anxious
Out the Door First So excited, I'll be out the door so fast to start enjoying things again	**Out There, Taking It Slow** I definitely will be out there, but taking it slower at first	**Wait and See** I am going to wait a week and see what happens	**Anxious** I am a bit anxious so will wait a few weeks	**Very Anxious** I am very anxious; it will be a while before I feel safe enough to go back to my normal activities

If we break this graphic into three components, we can really get a clearer picture of just how divided people were in their sentiment on reopening and getting back to life as we previously knew it.

- On the left, we have the two groups of people who knew for a fact they were going to get right back to life in the outside world. The difference between them was more about degrees of comfort than fear or anxiety. The "First Out the Door" group were going to proceed like the pandemic never happened and hit all of their favorite establishments. The "Out There, Taking It Slow" group was right alongside their counterparts, only they were going to be a bit more selective about where to go. For some it might have only been to church and the supermarket, while for others it could have been the mall and movie theaters. Regardless of their destinations, neither group wanted to wait a minute more.
- The middle-of-the-road group was the "Taking It Slow" folks. These are people who desperately wanted to get back out there but said they needed about a week of businesses open again before being comfortable enough to join the early adopters. This was very much a wait-and-see mentality. If everything seemed to be going well with no backslides, then it was their turn. People in this group might have been divided on their feelings about the First Out the Door group, ranging from jealousy over these early groups' ability to enjoy these experiences first to resentment towards that group for being a bit irresponsible.
- On the far right of the graphic, we have the two groups of consumers who were much less motivated to get back to normal and were more prone to thinking about what the new normal would look like. The more moderate of the two were the "Anxious" folks who still wanted to enjoy the activities that were taken away but needed a few weeks to sit back and see what happened before feeling confident enough to do so. Then there were the "Very Anxious" people who could not even put a timeframe on when they would be comfortable enough to go out. These two groups to varying degrees still harbor some anxiety over being in large groups and likely will for some time.

So, let's pause a minute.
Thinking back to March 2020, which segment did you most relate to?
What about December 2020, during the first surge?
What about Summer of 2021?
Did your attitudes fluctuate as time went on?
What about your behaviors? Did they change as time went on?

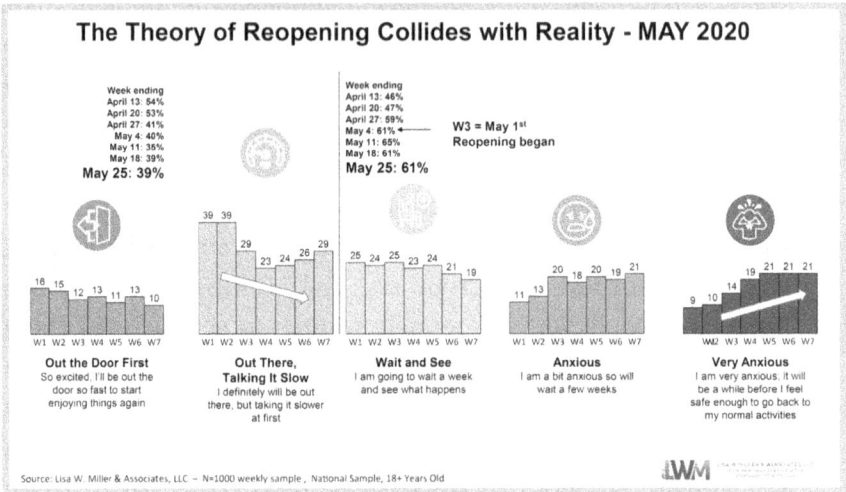

The Theory of Reopening Collides with Reality - MAY 2020

Out the Door First
So excited. I'll be out the door so fast to start enjoying things again

Out There, Talking It Slow
I definitely will be out there, but taking it slower at first

Wait and See
I am going to wait a week and see what happens

Anxious
I am a bit anxious so will wait a few weeks

Very Anxious
I am very anxious. It will be a while before I feel safe enough to go back to my normal activities

Source: Lisa W. Miller & Associates, LLC – N=1000 weekly sample , National Sample, 18+ Years Old

4. MESSAGING: LEADING WITH JOY, REASSURING WITH SAFETY

Despite all of the anticipation and excitement, most were still not ready when the doors opened, as I mentioned earlier. Honestly, we probably shouldn't have been surprised when the people didn't return in droves. So, while it seemed to be an unexpected response to reopening at the time, it's easy to look back now and understand why it should have been perfectly predictable. It wasn't because we didn't have a filter; we just weren't looking at it through the right lens of joy vs. fear and the re-entry segmentation framework.

As operators went into survival mode, safety protocols were "top of mind" as reopenings were mapped out. Keeping employees and customers safe was paramount. At the time, there was the early belief that the virus could be spread from person to person by touching surfaces. We would see public officials telling us not to touch surfaces and then rub our eyes or scratch our nose, or risk contracting the virus, then seconds later, they did that exact thing they told us not to do. Social media had a field day with that.

Below is just a short list of the types of changes operators were making and communicating, and of course, I was quantifying the appeal of all of them in my surveys to see if they would drive people back to restaurants.

2020 Operator Safety Measures

- CONTROLLED STORE ENTRY/EXIT
- CAPACITY LIMITS
- SAFETY GREETERS
- EQUIPMENT/SURFACES "CLEAN" WIPE DOWNS
- SOCIAL DISTANCING MANDATES
- PLEXIGLASS BARRIERS
- HAND SANITIZER
- SELF-CHECKOUT LINES AND AT THE TABLE
- IN-STORE MASKING AND MONITORING
- REINFORCING MESSAGES OF CONCERN AND CARE

LWM

When customers returned, new safety protocols were in place
Foley, Florida - Photo by Lisa W. Miller

For the consumers who did show up in those early days, they walked into a completely foreign experience that sometimes felt like you were on another planet – nothing like the experience before the pandemic. John Cywinski and I exchanged stories about this. John recalled, "You walk in, and you have to be sort of coached through it. Do we have to wear masks? Yes. I can't sit at all the tables because some of the tables are off-limits. Are you going to touch a reusable physical menu? No, we're going to give you a paper disposable menu or you can use a QR code. The whole thing was different. And servers wearing gloves?" Silverware was handed to you with a napkin. There were added plexiglass dividers between tables and sometimes on a table dividing an individual table.

After studying the data, I began to notice a predictable pattern:

- The "First Out the Door" and "Out the Door, Taking It Slow" segments were significantly _more_ likely to be dining out already, yet they were significantly _less_ interested in the safety protocols.
- And then the inverse was also true, the "Anxious/Very Anxious" segments were significantly _less_ likely to be dining out, yet they were significantly _more_ interested in the safety protocols.

Yet, at the time, many operators were sending emails to loyalty members, running TV commercials, and updating websites, all touting safety protocols because that was thought to be the key to the kingdom to bring back customer traffic. Ring a bell?

Basically, the communication hierarchy of messaging was upside down for many brands. They were leading with safety, which was essentially falling on deaf ears for the people who were actually going out. That's when I coined the phrase, "Lead with Joy. Reassure with Safety."

John and Applebee's exemplified this, a topic that we will cover in great detail later.

John shared his thoughts: "For those early customers, it was liberating and celebratory for them to be back dining out. Anecdotally, they were splurging more and tipping more in appreciation of the servers." It was joyful for the "First Out the Door" and "Out the Door, Taking It Slow" segments.

A LITTLE TENSION RELIEF, PLEASE
ENTER "DR. SAMMY TIZER"

As customers were walking back into dining rooms across America, many leaders mentioned experiencing and seeing this odd tension between joy and fear on the customers' faces. I always talked about "leading with joy and reassuring with safety." Jack Gibbons and his team at FB Society brought this to life in the early days of the pandemic, knowing that his restaurant customers wanted to have fun but also feel safe. It certainly was unconventional, but honestly, it was exactly what the doctor ordered.

Imagine walking into a Sixty Vines, Ida Claire, Whiskey Cake, or any other of their restaurant brands, and you encounter Dr. Sammy Tizer. Every FB Society restaurant had a Dr. Sammy Tizer. Jack recalled, "The fear was palpable in the restaurants, and we felt we needed to lighten it up a bit. So, we put a busser in a doctor's smock, a white lab jacket, and all he or she did was sanitize. Yeah, there was fear, but you gotta have a sense of humor."

5. EXPLAINING THE Q2 2021 RESTAURANT BOOM

You might recall that the second quarter of 2021 saw a boom in traffic. This quarter was nothing short of miraculous for the restaurant industry. Did you know that this spike in recovery was driven by the Anxious/Very Anxious segments FINALLY beginning to dine out again? Previously, their pent-up demand was high but until joy was greater than fear, that door was locked. After the holiday Delta surge settled down, this group cautiously put their toes back into the world of dining out. However, expectations were high and patience was low, which was the foundation of the customer behavior issues to come.

6. BRINGING FORWARD THE VOICES OF THE CONSUMERS

There are countless insights from other industry veterans who were in the trenches with both employees and customers who were experiencing the stress of the Covid-era language. But for the purposes of seeing the true dichotomy between fear and joy, it would be more appropriate to see how the average consumer felt about and dealt with the tension. These comments were collected during the same time period as the CEO interviews I conducted. There are no right or wrong answers on this, simply an acknowledgment of how different people felt and how those feelings had an impact on the economic recovery.

THE NEED FOR JOY PROPELLED PEOPLE FORWARD

"I miss people that I will not have seen for at least two months, and I miss getting to leave my home and walk around stores for fun."

Believe it or not, the consumer who shared that quote with me was coming from a place of joy and not fear. Yes, they were expressing sadness at some of the things they missed during the pandemic, but overall, the joy associated with being able to get back to doing those activities outweighed any sadness or fear. It boils down to a mindset as unique to each of us as our fingerprints. This is where much of the tension built up, individually and as a community. How individuals prioritized what was more important — staying safe inside due to fear or getting back to living but potentially placing yourself and others in danger — showed us that no two people were the same and explained why it has taken a long time to unwind the pent-up demand.

"I need a pedicure, I need to get my eyebrows waxed, I want to go to the beach, I want to see my family."

There is an interesting nugget reflected by the word choices for this particular consumer. Where there is a dichotomy between fear and joy, there also seems to be a separate dichotomy between needs and wants. We learned earlier that self-care and getting back to a salon ranked very high on the list of things people would do first once the economy reopened. The use of *need* in this context of pedicures and eyebrow waxing just reinforces how important those services were to certain people. And while this person classified going to the beach and seeing family as *wants,* there are many others who thrive off ocean air and human connection who might have viewed these activities as needs and the self-care as wants. Once again, no two people shared identical experiences during the pandemic.

FEAR HELD PEOPLE BACK AND CHANGED THEM

"I don't think the virus will magically disappear; I think it will be at increased risk for many months, maybe even years. Just by looking at the news, it is going to take a while before things get back to normal."

As you can see from the quote, when it came to fear, consumers had no reservations in expressing why they were anxious. Some of it had to do with their own preconceptions of what the words 'virus' and 'pandemic' meant, but much of it came back to the information (and misinformation) endlessly circulating around the media. When this information overload combines with one's own ingrained beliefs and the viewpoint of their social circle, it becomes hard for anyone to move past it.

"Exercising new habits of keeping away from people and seeking non-peak shopping hours and possibly wearing face coverings even during warmer months led to my anxiety."

This anxiety led to a shift in consumer behavior on multiple levels. While the most obvious was evident in desolate shopping malls and shuttered stores, some of it was much more obscure. Some started to switch sides of the street when walking if another person was approaching them. Others would tuck their heads down or pull the mask (which became a symbol of safety) just a little tighter to ensure no germs could slip by. It became downright nerve-racking to be constantly thinking about how you would have to react if placed into an uncomfortable social situation.

LESSONS LEARNED

What did we learn from this delicate balance between fear and joy?

1. SEGMENTATION AND MESSAGING MATTERS

When we thought we were ready to venture out, we came to the startling realization that many of us were not as ready to get back out there as we thought we were. But if we think back to the language of Covid and all of the messaging to which we were subjected, this shouldn't come as a surprise. That messaging continued from businesses when their doors opened, leading with all of the safety protocols they were putting in place instead of with the joyful experiences they could provide, which is what consumers really needed to hear in order to overcome the fear. The consumers who were the first out the door were going out regardless of safety protocols or mask mandates and could not care less what procedures were being followed.

What was a well-intentioned effort at putting people's minds at ease backfired for many brands. Those who were anxious or afraid about coming back out saw this advertising as a way of reinforcing the reality of the virus still being around and a real threat. If businesses were going to such great lengths to be "safe," then it stood to reason it was not safe otherwise. If any step in the safety measures was missed or corners were cut, the consumer would be in immediate danger. It was just better to stay at home and wait it out a little longer. If the messaging had been more focused on what the consumer wanted instead of what the company wanted to portray, we would have seen more adoption faster.

2. WHEN JOY BECAME GREATER THAN FEAR, THE ECONOMY REBOUNDED

Based on everything we have learned from the data in this and the earlier chapters, it might be hard to believe we could ever get back to a place where joy outweighed fear once again. But sometimes it only takes a singular event where people can unite and rally together in a way that overlooks the fear being shoved down our throats. That event just happened to be the holiday season in late November and December of 2021, or what I like to call a "joy holiday." Our data predicted consumers would come back out to brick-and-mortar stores to experience the joy of the holiday season, and while everyone thought I was crazy back then, my insight turned out to be right. People returned to stores and the scales were tilting back to joy.

3. PUSHING FORWARD, NOT BACKWARD

The same goes for today as it did in the early days of the pandemic – maybe even more so. Also, from a marketing perspective, one major lesson learned is that your audience should always come first. This might seem like common sense, but many companies missed this memo. They were sending out messages focused on what *they* as marketers and businesses, were doing to make things "safer" instead of thinking about how this would truly benefit *consumers*.

However, our next point is that consumers leading the economic recovery were really over all the safety talk – it was irrelevant to them at that point. Those consumers didn't want to hear that things were shut down again when they were ready to go out. In fact, it was the opposite of what they wanted. Unintended consequences can come from poor messaging.

Yet, according to more recent findings, 25% of Americans in November 2022 are still concerned and are anxious about Covid. Are you reminding customers about your safety procedures? Again, from an operator standpoint, we've moved on; we're not even talking about it anymore. But there's a missed chance to do that now when people aren't even asking for it. Those are things that, just from a fundamental standpoint, aren't being delivered right now. From a pandemic perspective, hopefully, this never happens again, but if more variants come around, we need to lead with joy and reassure people with messages about safety. Ask yourself, are you really executing against that today?

THE CUSTOMER ISN'T ALWAYS RIGHT

"Everyone wants to know why customer service has gone to hell in a handbasket. I want to know why customer behavior has gone to hell in a handbasket."

– Brené Brown

O VERNIGHT, THE PANDEMIC changed the face of business. Yet, there was an undercurrent of consumer frustration and tension brewing that took longer to become visible. Unbeknownst to us, as the months of lockdown turned into years, our social skills were among the more significant casualties. Some would venture to say, as consumers we've lost our minds. The things that were designed to protect us ended up scaring us more instead. And in the process, we turned on each other.

We've all seen it in the news and maybe experienced it firsthand – the seemingly countless instances of rude customer behavior. Did they really need to make a server cry because their hamburger wasn't cooked correctly? What about the incident where a customer threw hot soup on an employee because the lid had melted? Come on, people, really? And it's not just an uptick in unruly behavior in restaurants. Airport personnel, hotel staff, and retail employees have all reported increased instances of scuffles, rude comments, and other disruptive behavior from customers.

Looking back, it was perfectly predictable, but while we were living it, it was like a fuse blew and set off a chain reaction we are still reeling from today. Bad customer behavior is terrible for business. Not only does it negatively impact the bottom line, but it also takes a toll on employees' morale and job satisfaction. In an era when businesses are struggling to find and retain top talent, that's something no company can afford.

1. HOW DID WE GET HERE?

The short answer is that throughout the two-plus years of the pandemic, we were on an emotional rollercoaster. It honestly felt like a bit of bait and switch of anticipation to return to our normal activities and then the disappointment that the activities weren't quite the same when we did show up. Plus, there was an endless cycle of businesses opening and shutting down, then reopening. It was exhausting.

We remembered and craved the experiences that were taken away. At first, the isolation from our friends, family, and co-workers seemed like a nice respite from the world but that quickly turned into pandemic fatigue. We all just were a bit out of practice when it came to interacting with other people.

Attitudinal differences between us that might have gone unnoticed and tolerated became amplified during the pandemic. At the most fundamental level, there was a massive difference between the concern and the lack of concern about the Covid virus itself. Even as early as May of 2020, the attitudinal differences were stark in our First Out the Door segment vs. our Very Anxious segment, as evidenced by the chart below. Regardless of which side of the continuum you occupied, there was a growing lack of tolerance or understanding of the "other" side. The longer the lockdown lasted, the more the many inequalities grew and highlighted differences in how we not only viewed the pandemic but how we experienced it.

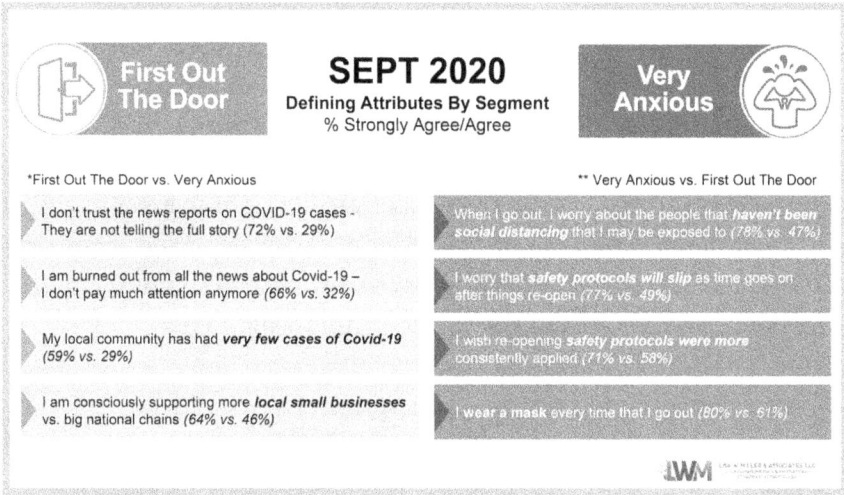

First Out The Door

SEPT 2020
Defining Attributes By Segment
% Strongly Agree/Agree

Very Anxious

*First Out The Door vs. Very Anxious

** Very Anxious vs. First Out The Door

I don't trust the news reports on COVID-19 cases - They are not telling the full story (72% vs. 29%)

When I go out, I worry about the people that *haven't been social distancing* that I may be exposed to (78% vs. 47%)

I am burned out from all the news about Covid-19 – I don't pay much attention anymore (66% vs. 32%)

I worry that *safety protocols will slip* as time goes on after things re-open (77% vs. 49%)

My local community has had *very few cases of Covid-19* (59% vs. 29%)

I wish re-opening *safety protocols were more* consistently applied (71% vs. 58%)

I am consciously supporting more *local small businesses* vs. big national chains (64% vs. 46%)

I wear a mask every time that I go out (80% vs. 61%)

LWM

2. CONSUMERS SHOWED UP ANGRIER

The anticipation and expectations were high, yet patience was low.

When the doors finally opened, the restaurant experience looked and felt completely different. It felt foreign and surreal. Everyone was masked up. Wait times actually increased despite fewer customers due to capacity mandates where every other table was left empty. The experience was stripped down to the core, leaving customers questioning whether it was worth it.

- Reduced staff
- Reduced menus
- Reduced hours
- Reduced seating capacity
- Menus morphed to QR Code Menus
- Higher prices
- Favorite items were cut or out of stock

It wasn't the joyful experience that we were hoping for, and it shouldn't have been a surprise that frustrations began mounting.

Masking and vaccination mandates fueled more confrontations.

The vaccines that were supposed to make us feel more comfortable and confident about re-entering the economy ended up not being the economic boost in the arm that was promised. In fact, they became a contentious issue that divided the country. Municipalities around the country mandated proof of vaccinations to enter business establishments, resulting in fewer people than expected venturing back out. The vaccinated didn't want to be around the unvaccinated, and the unvaccinated didn't want to be told what to do.

Whether learning to reread facial expressions or remembering how to engage in small talk, in my opinion, we've all lost a bit of our social finesse. And unfortunately, it seems simply removing a mask isn't enough to help us regain those skills. There are several reasons for this. First, masks made it harder to read facial expressions, which made it difficult to gauge someone's emotions. Masks also tended to muffle some voices, especially for those who are soft-spoken by nature, and it became difficult to communicate. Lastly, the fact that many who would have normally interacted in person were now working remotely made it easier to avoid resolving conflicts in person. Ill will just festered. Countless videos emerged of unmasked patrons filming their interactions with employees who were asking them to comply with the mask policy. Some consumers went so far as to taunt employees in the most obnoxious ways to "test the rules." They would get their cameras out as if to taunt a scuffle, and video what happened.

Stephen Colbert even did a skit on his show, Late Night with Stephen Colbert, based on my research spoofing just how bad this customer behavior got and how customers were filming employees' interactions.[8]

---

[8] "Stephen Colbert Rude Customer Behavior - "Research Says... "." YouTube, February 17, 2022. https://www.youtube.com/watch?v=-nA8EW2JpiM.

Our frontline workers were literally having to deal with this day in and day out.

3. FRONTLINE EMPLOYEES SAID THEY'D HAD ENOUGH

> *"Be kind or leave"*
> – Chris Sirianni, Owner, Brewerie at Union Station

During the pandemic, for those who kept their job while others were being furloughed, it was a blessing and a curse. Stress was high and with fewer customers coming through the doors, the potential earnings (in a tip-based business) shrank. You were often greeted each day with the same amount of work, if not more, yet with a fraction of the resources. The workers who kept showing up despite this were often resentful of those choosing not to work or those on corporate staff who were given the work-from-home option. Frontline retail and restaurant workers put themselves in harm's way each and every day they clocked in, while many support center colleagues comfortably worked from home.

After months of unruly customer behavior, many frontline workers concluded that it just wasn't "worth it" to show up anymore. The bad customer behavior accelerated the labor shortages, which turned into a self-fulfilling prophecy. As the customers became more unruly, many hourly workers started to find out from their unemployed colleagues that there was more money to be made staying home rather than working. And for those who remained in the workforce, there was a mass exodus from the restaurant industry to jobs like delivery where there was less stress, flexible hours, and better pay.

As the Covid-19 pandemic progressed, many businesses took drastic measures to protect their employees and ensure labor shortages were not in their future. One of the most common was offering "Covid pay" – a daily stipend for employees who chose to stay home if they felt slightly ill. While this may have limited the virus's spread, it also created a unique set of challenges for employers. It became difficult to distinguish between genuine illness and those who were simply taking advantage of the situation. People weren't necessarily quitting, but mass callouts did not do much to alleviate staffing challenges.

The Brewerie at Union Station went so far as to take matters into their own hands when a sign was posted saying, "Be Kind or Leave." The simple sign on the front door, created by the business' owner Chris Sirianni, spoke volumes about how bad things had become, yet on the positive, it was a powerful statement of support for his employees. The sign went on to say, "many people in this building have been through hell and back this past year. If you can't treat them with the same courtesy and respect that they give to you, we kindly ask that you take your business elsewhere. Our staff is our family and they deserve better."

Photo courtesy of The Brewerie at Union Station

4. ALL WAS NOT LOST; THERE WAS STILL GRATITUDE AND JOY

> *"Treat everyone with politeness and kindness, not because they are nice, but because you are."*
> – Roy T. Bennett, *The Light in the Heart*

When reflecting on all of the outrageous incidents, it is refreshing to remember that this unruly behavior wasn't always the case. There were customers who were genuinely grateful for the businesses and their employees who continued to serve them even though the experience was far from perfect. In the beginning, customers gave some grace for those imperfections as we all were fumbling through new experiences together.

John Cywinski recalled from the early days how consumers ordered more food than they normally would and anecdotally, they tipped more generously. It was the customers' little indulgences that they perhaps missed over a really long period of time. "Guests were so thankful to be dining out again, actually sitting down at a restaurant, not going through the drive-thru. Consumers would indulge a bit more, having a drink or ordering a dessert," John explained. That gratitude was expressed on both sides of the counter, or table, as well. As Kelli Valade, CEO of Denny's Corporation told me, "We were grateful for those on our team who continued showing up every day. It would have been easy for many more to stay home."

This sentiment of gratitude wasn't only among customers; it was among the business partners as well. Robin Blanchette, President and CEO of Norton Creative advertising agency, spoke to me about "feeling like the pandemic uncovered people's true characters," and it wasn't specific to the restaurant industry by any means. There were instances of renters doing everything in their power to make payments to their landlords while others took full advantage of the emergency legislation that prevented evictions. The same translated to business owners, some of whom proactively tried renegotiating invoices with their suppliers, and others who adopted an attitude of "If I'm not getting paid, neither are you." It was because of her convictions and the way she handled her own clients that she received personal phone calls from the likes of Golden Corral CEO, Lance Trenary, to express how grateful he was for her support and being a good partner.

"I think how so many of us were able to work together up and down the food chain is an integral part of how we all made it this far," Robin added. From where she sat, Covid highlighted the importance of transparency and honesty in all relationships. Those factors, along with grace between members of the value chain, were what facilitated everyone being able to work together in the first place. The decisions we make have ripple effects across lives, businesses, and industries. Robin recalled a time when one of her lenders called to express how they felt her company as a whole executed better and navigated more adeptly than anyone else in their portfolio. The driving force behind that sentiment was their constant transparency and always delivering on what was promised.

LESSONS LEARNED

1. RETHINK CONVENTIONAL WISDOMS, THEY MAY NO LONGER APPLY

If we learned nothing else from this drastic change in behavior on the part of consumers, it was having to rethink the validity of traditionally ingrained beliefs. "The customer is always right" is a saying usually embraced by the unruliest and most entitled consumers who hide behind it as an excuse to justify their behavior. Prior to the pandemic, many service-related businesses would go above and beyond to uphold that belief and make concessions in a customer's favor even when they were in the wrong. But as the months and years dragged on, we came to realize that the customer is not always right.

2. BE A PART OF THE SOLUTION, NOT THE PROBLEM

Human nature often drives us to look outward for the sources of problems and point fingers at others rather than acknowledging the role we may have played in creating them. While it's true we as individuals cannot be held responsible for the negative actions of others, there is always room for introspection. The labor shortages we have been experiencing over the last few months, especially in the retail and hospitality sectors, cannot be blamed entirely on those employees not wanting to work. We, the general public as consumers, must take responsibility for our own actions and recognize how we have contributed to the problem. Doing that is the first step in realizing we can also be part of the solution.

3. MAKE SURE TO HAVE YOUR EMPLOYEES' BACKS

Beyond what we learned about consumer behavior, there were learnings for management teams as it pertained to dealing with their employees. The path forward would not be anything like it was in the past, with hierarchical structures and rules written in stone. This new environment gave birth to a new sense of awareness from frontline workers who could now see just how important they were to the organization. Leaders were going to have to focus on listening, empathy, and flexibility going forward if they were to have any hope of retaining their talent.

Simply listening to and empathizing with employees is only the first part of the equation, though. An organization can invest countless dollars in exploring the needs of employees as deeply as they do the needs of their customers, but it needs to be reinforced with action. Employees need to know it is not just lip service when employers speak about having their backs and that they will be defended if it comes down to an unsavory customer experience. While delivering an exceptional customer experience still remains the goal, it must start and end with our biggest resource – our people.

DECISIVE LEADERSHIP

"Be grateful for adversity, for it forces the human spirit to grow."

– Jim Rohn

A s I spoke with leaders from around the industry, I wanted them to also reflect on what it was like to navigate their businesses through the pandemic. In listening to them share their stories and insights, a pervasive theme emerged. It was decisive leadership.

They didn't call it that themselves, but it was so clear to me that these leadership stories needed to be told. The struggles of the frontline were well documented during the pandemic, yet these stories from the top were not. As Jack Gibbons put it, "You're either the leader who ran into the pandemic or ran away from it." Jack was right. The leaders of the restaurant industry ran into the pandemic to ensure the industry not only survived but would emerge stronger on the other side. Leaders reflected that they couldn't be paralyzed by fear; they just couldn't let that happen. They had to measure and make decisions. They had to act, be flexible, and be nimble. It's remarkable how far we've come, and more importantly, how we got here through decisive leadership.

All of the insights in this chapter are from the viewpoints of the leaders who spent their days (and many nights as well) discerning the data available to make very hard decisions. That's not to say that all of the decisions made were well-received, but I believe those who acted quickly and decisively fared better in the long term than those who flip-flopped with each new piece of information that came out.

It was humbling to see the leaders' vulnerability as they opened up and shared personal stories of shouldering incredible untold pressures, doing the best they could with what they had. With the number of people relying on them, they had no choice but to exude confidence and calmness on the outside while inwardly hoping they had made the right calls. As I listened to the tough conversations about furloughing staff and the emotional stories of kindness and generosity of spirit and even the hilarious stories about operators adding a roll of toilet paper to a to-go order, my emotions ran the gamut.

And so it began, head down in the weeds 24/7.

Most of their stories started something like this….

In March, it was surreal because you are hearing all of these stories in the news and don't really know the severity. But you do know it's starting to cause disruption in your business because your sales are becoming erratic. And then your legal department comes in every single day, telling you about a different mandate that is forcing you to operate differently. And all the while, you're starting to have your employee base asking questions. It's like the perfect storm. Your legal department doesn't really know what any of it means either. Yet as leaders, you still had to act and make decisions – some more conservative decisions and some more draconian than others.

Your sales are declining. Your team is like, "Whoa! What's going on?" Your stores went from operating at full capacity to completely closed in 30 days. Your stores are meant to be open. You have food, management teams, hourly employees, and you don't know when you are going to reopen, but you're trying to stay optimistic, right? Because you'd never seen yourself closed. We know how to get through hurricanes and other disasters, but we had no idea how long this would last.

If after reading those short paragraphs, you are feeling a little anxious or stressed, that's the point. Now, imagine actually living through it. This is what the many industry leaders faced on a daily basis.

1. TAKING OWNERSHIP SOLIDIFIED HOPE

Leaders had to learn to process new and changing information rapidly and be flexible in making decisions in the best interest of the company, employees, and customers. They were forced to pivot more quickly than ever before. Throughout my interviews, I saw that companies reflected on their businesses and assessed quickly where their strengths and weaknesses were.

Robin Blanchette echoed Anita Adams's sentiment about recognizing strengths and weaknesses. She took it a step further with a significant focus placed on leaning into strengths and remembering the specific value her company brought to its clients. "During the pandemic, I thought it was time for us to take ownership of what we were good at and be proud of it while standing on our own two feet."

Prior to Covid, Robin felt like her company as a whole had focused on humbly doing good work without chasing after any awards or recognition. Most would agree humility is a good characteristic for any person or company, but not necessarily in every situation. When there is so much going wrong in the world all around you, celebrating any and all successes is vital to keeping people motivated and positive. It was out of remembering what the company was good at and good for that executives and other employees found the hope that allowed them to endure the never-ending challenges.

2. CHANGING REOPENING GOAL LINES

There is no doubt in my mind that without these instances of decisive leadership, many of these companies would not have survived. Every leader I spoke with recounted the magnitude of simply staying on top of mandate variations from one location to the next. We already discussed how problematic this was on a macro level, but at the restaurant operational level, the things leadership teams had to deal with were sheer insanity. Seating capacity could bounce around from 25% – 75% from what felt like one day to the next. It was impossible to consistently have the right balance of staff and supplies to handle the volume on any given day. Can you imagine going from operating at 25% capacity and going back to carry-out only overnight, while juggling the staffing model and food waste at the same time?

It might be clear from all of the challenges we just discussed how impactful these leaders who stepped up were, but it's also quite humbling when listening to the experiences from their point of view. Anita once told me, "I just knew we needed to make sure people were going to be able to survive in the face of the new information we were getting on a daily basis." Like many leaders, Anita knew it was her job to deal with ambiguity, but this was more like ambiguity on steroids. Literally, every decision that was made yesterday could be questioned today and completely changed tomorrow.

How operators experienced Covid varied dramatically, just like it did for the consumers. Black Bear Diners are geographically dispersed across the country yet heavily concentrated in California and the West, where some of the lockdowns were most severe and prolonged. They were living in two different worlds. While Texas and Oklahoma were marching towards full capacity, in California, every week a map came out with a rainbow of colors showing how much occupancy was allowed – which varied county by county. "The California guys need all of us right now, so we've got to be that much better in other diners to help these guys who are struggling," was exactly what she explained to the field to rally them. It built an appreciation of being a larger company, and that they were all banding together.

3. CHALLENGING COMMUNICATIONS AND THE INEVITABLE FURLOUGHS

One of the biggest decisions any leader had to contend with was also one of the hardest. It was unfortunate, but all had to furlough or lay off people. Topline revenue was slashed with expenses still coming in, making the balance sheet bleak. Leaders had to be as clear as they could with the information they had. How messages cascaded down was starkly different during the pandemic than it usually was. Instead of the typical hierarchical communication, leaders many times communicated down the line themselves. They were compelled to deliver these tough conversations without middlemen. Messages had to be sharp and contain these three components:

1) This is what we're doing.
2) This is why we're doing it.
3) This is what it means to you.

Leaders had to comfort many grown men and women breaking down and crying about the uncertainty for their families. Leaders spoke about how all people wanted during the most challenging times was to have this kind of emotional connection with them. This was unchartered waters and very emotional. Leaders recounted how these were the hardest days of their lives.

But despite the bad or unexpected that may have come with some of these decisions, everyone was also looking to leadership for reassurance when questions arose about how long it would last. Employees had questions:

- *OK, I'm furloughed. For how long?*
- *You're asking me to take a pay cut. OK, for how long?*
- *Is my family still covered by insurance?*
- *How long do you think it will take to get back to 100% capacity?*

Unfortunately, leaders didn't have all of the answers. It would have been easy for them to pretend everything was going to be fine, but in the long run it would have damaged relationships with the employees. Much like no one expects anyone to have all the answers all the time, employees knew there were limitations in what management teams knew or could swear to. Honest bad news or no news at all proved to be better than telling people what they wanted to hear. People needed transparency. Leaders were trading in all the equity they had built up in their reputation with their employees.

4. BALANCING UNCERTAIN STAFFING LEVELS AND CUSTOMER COUNTS

As the days, weeks, and months continued, it took a toll, personally impacting everyone within an organization in one way or another. Leaders needed to keep employees safe. There was daily talk about the number of callouts as managers and frontline employees contracted Covid or were concerned about exposure to co-workers, friends, or family members with Covid. This left an incredible load for those who did go to work to carry. At the end of the day in those early days, the number of employees who would show up was as uncertain as the number of customers to expect. Regional managers, directors of operations, and even restaurant support center staff were asked to take shifts to help the field. But the normal community support of being understaffed that one would see in the wake of a natural disaster waned over time during Covid when it became clear there was no end in sight to the pandemic. This set in motion a labor shortage crisis that is still an issue today and will ultimately take years to unwind.

5. FINDING APPRECIATION IN THE MOST UNEXPECTED PLACES

In the stress of it all, and the sometimes-constant barrage of change and difficult decisions and conversations, the leaders were taken aback by moments of kindness and appreciation towards them, often coming from the most unexpected places. Margo Manning gave her cell phone number out to anybody who asked for it. She remembered when furloughed employees would call just to thank her. Because of the layoff, they reconnected with their spouses, and they were afraid at first, but in the end, it was the biggest blessing for them. She recalled another specific story about an hourly kitchen employee: "I had a member of our kitchen team call me. He had been on the line with us for over eighteen years. I said, 'Hey, how are you doing? What can I do for you?' And he replied, 'I was just calling to check on you.' I started choking up. I had this man calling to check on me! I couldn't believe it!"

Anita Adams experienced something similar. "I'm calling these individuals and saying, 'I'm so sorry, but in light of what we're dealing with, I just cannot keep your position.' I remember two individuals saying, 'I'm so sorry you have to make these calls.' And you have to go on telling them you know they're no longer going to have a paycheck and at the same time they're empathetic to the position you are in. That's just moving."

Jack Gibbons and the team at FB Society wanted to find a way to give back to their furloughed associates while at the same time keeping them safe. He was concerned that with so much negativity happening most days, the team could only take so much. He wanted to move the team forward to thinking about something positive. At the time, Jack recalled, "We have all this food. We have people who want to do stuff. We just decided one night, let's turn it into a *Furlough Kitchen*."

From there the idea just grew. It started for just furloughed employees of FB Society, and then they opened it up to anyone furloughed. But it didn't stop there. Jack was getting calls from around the country to open up other Furlough Kitchens. "We pulled together these documents. It was the first time anyone ever created a franchise system with no franchise fees. It was like a franchise that was an anti-franchise." This is just one example of the commitment in the industry to keep feeding people.

There were countless stories of celebrations happening at the end of a crazy busy and short-handed shift. On the surface it sounds completely bonkers, right? So, why were people so happy up and down the ranks? It meant more people could be brought back on the schedule. It truly was something to celebrate. Leaders and frontline workers cheered alike.

6. CREATING UNTRADITIONAL SUPPORT NETWORKS

It is not common to see competitors in business coming together to work toward a common cause. With few exceptions, the success of one restaurant could be viewed as a direct threat to others in the same geographic region. There are examples like Restaurant Row in New York City where the concentration of restaurants actually helps to boost business for all, but even then, the individual establishments are not actively coordinating with one another. But the effects of Covid were so dire for the restaurant industry as a whole that this is exactly what many leaders decided to do.

Starlette Johnson, an industry leader who serves on several restaurant boards, summarized it like this, "We were fighting for our industry, not just for our company. I think that was really what happened. We weren't talking about crossing the line on sharing trade secrets about recipes or pricing, but instead what we could do to save our teams. What did we do to save our brands and what worked for everybody individually? There were several points along that timeline where competitors were reaching out asking how we were able to accomplish certain things. It was a very interesting, hectic, crazy, and stressful period. But it did bring out the best of each other in the industry."

With this type of open communication, competitors became supportive confidants – sharing ideas and solutions on a regular basis. There were a lot of leaders looking for support and guidance. Groups of restaurateurs who hardly ever communicated in the past put together collaborative phone calls. Leaders created an environment where they would get on the phone weekly, sometimes even nightly to discuss the issues of the day. It was a critical and important step that helped the industry come out of the pandemic.

LESSONS LEARNED

1. LEADING US BACK TO JOY TOOK COURAGE AND VULNERABILITY

I hope this brings to life the immense gratitude that is owed to the leaders who selflessly navigated an entire industry forward so all of us could find joy again in restaurants across America. Leaders are human too. They were uncertain. They were feeling upset and concerned but were compelled every day to keep going for everyone who depended on them. It's important to note that all of the leaders I spoke with were very humble in their role of this, and as good leaders do, they focused on the efforts of their teams, not themselves.

That said, leaders are used to having control and steering the ship. As the leader, they are the ones to say, "I've got this and I'm going to make everybody else feel OK." That is a hard burden to carry. Throughout the pandemic, leaders had to be comfortable with being uncomfortable just like the rest of us did. It was okay to say, "I don't have the answer. You don't have the answer, but we're going to figure it out together." And that they did.

2. REIMAGINING THE BUSINESS MADE IT STRONGER

Leaders had to completely reimagine and re-envision how they ran their businesses. They had to figure out how they could do it in real-time going forward. Given all the mandates, they had no choice but to create new concepts, experiences, and business models underneath the old brand names. This was quite different for a leader who is used to saying – "I'm going to create a plan. I'm going to work the plan. I'll adjust the plan." Covid wasn't that. It was much bigger, much deeper. And no one in this industry, including the leaders, could have been prepared for what happened in March of 2020.

3. FORESHADOWING OF THE GREAT REASSESSMENT TO COME

By March of 2022, my broader research suggested a tipping point was about to happen across the country. It was a time to pause and reflect on what was important after the frenzy of the previous two years. It wasn't the "Great Resignation" but more the "Great Reassessment." We will cover that in more depth later in the book, yet in my humble opinion, it might be one of the profound positives coming out of the pandemic. For leaders and everyone up and down organizations, it was no different. Many paused their personal and professional goals for two non-stop years of running hard, trying to make the best strategic choices, working to save and create jobs.

ACCELERATED INNOVATION, BUT CAN IT LAST?

"So, the future doesn't get better by hope it gets better by design."

– Jim Rohn

T HE SPEED AT which companies innovated during the pandemic was nothing short of mind-blowing. Technology enabled off-premises dining, menu reductions, menu innovations, you name it - and it happened at record speed. And let's not forget all this innovation happened with skeleton staffs.

The innovation itself, the "what" was accomplished, has been well documented, yet this has not been the case with the "how." So that got me thinking:

- With backs against the wall, "how" would decisions be made so quickly and boldly?
- What was the secret sauce that enabled the industry to pivot so quickly?

- Can we capture these insights to replicate this accelerated innovation again and again in the post-Covid world?

So, it's time to talk about "how" all that innovation happened. As part of this chapter, you'll find questions throughout that I'd like you to ponder with me.

1. THE THREE F's OF FOCUS DROVE SPEED

Sara Rosenberg Bittorf, Chief Strategy Officer of TGI Fridays, captured the essence with one word – "focus." We talked briefly about focus earlier, but I wanted to go deeper here. She explained a philosophy she developed many years prior to the pandemic that eloquently described her three F's of focus. Her approach helped the team at Fridays navigate the pandemic.

The Three F's of FOCUS

a) **F**igure Out What Matters
b) Do **F**ewer Things Better
c) Do **F**irst Things First

As I listened and learned from many leaders about "how" they pivoted, I found examples of each of her three F's.

The Three Fs of FOCUS
From Sara Rosenberg Bittorf

Figure Out What Matters   Do **F**ewer Things Better   Do **F**irst Things First

a) <u>Figure out what matters</u>:

During Covid, companies quickly figured out what mattered. That was easy and crystal clear – keep the lights on, as we discussed earlier. It was survival mode. Leaders needed to figure out how to make money when dining rooms were closed amidst the changing mandates and regulations; plus, they needed to determine how to take care of employees. At that moment in time, the rest became background noise and didn't matter.

During Covid, brands were doing one thing, and if there's anything that we've learned, it is that the value of focus cannot be underestimated. Now, I'm not naive enough to say that in a highly competitive world coming out of Covid you can only do one thing. We have to do more things than that to drive the business, but two-plus years later, there's been scope creep compounded still by being short-staffed. It's easy to fall back into old habits and lose focus.

b) <u>Do fewer things better</u>:

Margo Manning, former COO of Dave & Busters, recalled her approach when it came to building the reopening plans during those first 30 days. "Our meetings were one hundred percent focused on reopening. And the only way out of this was going to be if we reopened stronger." Leaders had to look deep into the dark corners of their businesses. They identified and explored <u>all</u> the things that "weren't great about Dave & Busters, inside and out, and no matter how big or small," and took away those issues to come out stronger on the other side. And, that they did.

c) <u>Do first things first</u>:

Innovation and menu work has always provided the lifeblood of restaurants, keeping brands relevant and current, yet innovation processes can be long and arduous.

As we discussed earlier, Tobin Ellis produced the Hospitality Relief Dashboard in record time to help the industry navigate the early days and weeks of the pandemic. As time went on, Tobin identified another gap facing the industry. He shared, "What would be useful now would be stories from the field with real concrete, meaty examples of how to win in this insane world." He researched and packaged up not just innovation examples from the U.S. but from around the world. The outcome was a ninety-six-page masterpiece of creativity to inspire restaurants and bars alike of what was possible during impossible times. As part of this work, he also shared my Journey Back to Joy research consumer insights to ground businesses in delivering joy not fear. From page 1, "What awaits you in the pages ahead is a curated collection of strategies and tactics from the field that are working that I wanted to put together after spending 18 years designing bars and restaurants and 30 years working (and playing) within them. A survival guide that represents a tiny slice of the best of who we can be and who we already are. Stay strong, find a way to make it fun, and keep the faith."

John Cywinski shared how complex the menu had been with 160 items. It became difficult to execute given the highly variable traffic counts and a much-reduced staff. John and his team made the tough call to cut 35% of the menu during the pandemic. "We took the menu down to ninety items in thirty days to reduce complexity." And then he joked, "That would have taken eighteen years before the pandemic!" They did it out of necessity to make the customer experience better through better execution.

ASK YOURSELF:

- *Figure out what matters*
  - *Are you relentlessly focusing on what matters most today to grow your business?*
  - *Is your team crystal clear on that top priority?*

- *Do fewer things better*
  - *Have you identified the company's top pain points, both internal and consumer-facing?*
  - *Are you continuously improving and removing these pain points?*

- *Do first things first*
  - *Are you doing first things first, or is everything a competing and urgent priority?*
  - *Are you allowing space for your team to focus on the top priority?*

---

2. THE TEXTBOOK INNOVATION PROCESS WAS REFRAMED

We've all heard the folklore of a mother who finds the strength to lift a car off her child, which is great symbolism for what many businesses did to stay alive. But the true way forward is more akin to the crowd of onlookers who rush over to help the mother lift the car. Teamwork was the way forward.

From a process standpoint, some of these next points may seem painfully obvious, yet are often overlooked. These are the gentle — or not-so-gentle — reminders to harness what enabled the massive innovation at the beginning of the pandemic. As with everything, creating new processes does take work, but the innovation success found during the pandemic demonstrates it can work.

"Houston, we have a problem" – everything was on the line and on the table

During Covid, ideas came from anywhere and everywhere. Teams gathered quickly to assess this new problem called Covid. It reminds me of the movie *Apollo 13* when the astronauts said, "Houston, we have a problem," and those on the ground went feverishly into action. They threw out on the table all of the available materials on the spacecraft to craft a solution to get the astronauts home safely. Every possible idea was on the table literally and figuratively, waiting to be discovered.

The openness and nimbleness of ideas considered during Covid were like nothing the industry had ever seen. Literally anyone from the frontline staff to the CEO could contribute to creating the solutions.

Are you inviting and embracing ideas from
all parts of the organization?

Failure was an option

There was an urgency to innovate because businesses had to, but under that urgency was passion to keep trying. To be clear, this statement is about trying new ideas, not failing as an organization. In the world of innovation "best practices," it is well known that innovative organizations encourage people to fail and fail often. Prior to the pandemic, companies that truly celebrated failures, appreciating what worked as much as what didn't work, were few and far between. Many aspired, but few really lived it.

And then came Covid.

Innovation failure was not only an option, but it was also vital during the pandemic. It didn't have to be perfect by any means. It was just "go time." Literally, every leader to whom I spoke mentioned this as a theme.

Are you still trying new things at record
speed, or has your process slowed?

Being nimble and innovative is second nature to Khanh Nguyen, founder and CEO of ZaLat Pizza, a Dallas-based Hot Concept as designated by Nation's Restaurant News. In talking with him, he shared several stories about their innovation in the early weeks and months. Keep in mind, unlike most casual dining brands, ZaLat Pizza was booming, so the brand was getting unprecedented new trial. To that end, Khanh saw an opportunity to launch new elevated pizzas that would solidify their brand position as the pizza zealots.

Where do you start? With the pepperoni pizza of course. Being zealots, Khanh recalled "Why don't we go all in on it? We're going to kill it, (it's) not just Pepperoni Lovers. Let's call it a masterclass. We're going to teach everybody a masterclass in the (art) of pepperoni pizza". From there, they had a design session to develop the recipe and the Masterclass Pizza immediately went to number one and stayed there.

But Khanh didn't stop innovating there. ZaLat also launched the Reaper Roulette pizza. Basically, one unmarked slice of pizza is hit with some incredibly spicy hot flavor. You don't know which one until you bite into it. Not only did that provide some entertainment value for the customers, it was also an add-on sale increasing margin to the bottom line.

By the way, did you know that vinegar is a better way to calm the heat from spicy food than milk? I learn something new every day!

Reaper Roulette Challenge. "Warning: this challenge is incredibly spicy!!! Super fun to play with family and friends though. Just be prepared. With this option, one unmarked slice of your pizza is NUCLEAR hot. #SpiceHack – table vinegar is way better to counteract spicy food than milk."

Reaper Roulette Challenge

Photo courtesy of ZaLat Pizza

3. WELL, COVID WAS JUST DIFFERENT; WE HAD NO CHOICE

To win today, the strategies have to be bigger; we can't stay where we are. When asking employees what happened in Covid, I often hear, "That was different. We had to survive; we had no choice. We wouldn't be here if we didn't do those crazy things."

During Covid, the 80/20 rule applied. There wasn't the time, the money, or the people to overthink anything. Companies had to just act and try, knowing some of it wouldn't work, but also knowing the consumers were going to be more accepting just to get things up and open for business.

Kelli Valade and I discussed that while at Black Box Intelligence, she would share with clients that they shouldn't lose sight of that sense of urgency. What if you woke up every day and said there wasn't any choice but to act fast? What would you do today? We don't want every employee to say that every day, but what if they did say something like that to remind themselves what got them to do things that fast?

How will you keep that passion and sense of urgency alive coming out of the pandemic, so the innovation doesn't wane?

LESSONS LEARNED

1. CAPTURE "HOW" YOU INNOVATED NOT THE "WHAT"

I am an innovator at heart. This innovation born from passion and urgency helped many establishments survive, but it was also aimed at providing joy for whatever patrons were brave enough to come out. It is one thing to provide a joyful experience on a regular day, but it can mean something entirely different when there is so much uncertainty.

We can't lose sight of what we learned about the innovation process during the pandemic. Looking back, just the idea that you could innovate faster than you ever imagined is an invaluable lesson. And honestly, the foundation of "how" innovation happened during the pandemic isn't that farfetched. It mirrors closely the known best practices of innovative companies. The difference back then is we had no choice. Now, we are back to having a choice.

Now is the time to get everything down on paper and study it within your organization before memories fade. Take it back to your teams and discuss all the ways it can be harnessed and improved going forward. It is time to decide whether you are going to go back to the "old way of doing things" or whether you will continue to embrace the principles of change that saw you through one of the darkest periods in the last 100 years.

2. CREATE A CULTURE OF INNOVATION

Nothing is ever perfect. Covid may have been the impetus for rapid change within the business models, but it was also the foreshadowing of what was to come for those who couldn't pivot and keep up. It's hard, I know. But as leaders, we have to enable this culture of innovation to thrive and live on.

- To go back to old habits at this stage of the game would erase all of the success and survival stories.
- To stay relevant with consumers and ahead of competitors, the key is to keep a foot on the gas pedal of innovation and continuous improvement.

So, the challenge today is to harness the learning and retain the innovation culture created by the pandemic:

- Can your decision-making be quicker?
- Can you take bolder risks?
- Are you encouraging and embracing ideas from everyone?
- Are you trying to make it perfect before trying it?

VALUE EQUATION REDEFINED: WHY JOY MATTERS

"Consumers' needs didn't change; how we had to deliver them changed."

– Barry McGowan

W HY DOES JOY matter in the value equation? Joy is the emotional differentiator in the food sea of sameness. Yes, there are some distinct and craveable menu offerings out there, yet, let's be honest, the food alone isn't the differentiator; it's the experience that differentiates. We know the magic happens at the moment of the bite along with the total sensory enjoyment of the full experience. That's why consumers look to see and hear the sizzle of the fajitas go by, the "oooh-ahhh" of a delicious dessert going by, and even the tableside preparation finishing off foods, all the while the server is smiling and engaging with the table – "taking care" of the customers. The food is the center stage of the theater, and servers are our cast members delivering joy – all together, it makes the experience "worth it."

I challenge you to think about this. In every meeting… every decision needs to be contemplated against this filter – is this decision going to help or hurt in making the experience "worth it?" If the decisions being made are not helping the customer experience, you are likely eroding your value equation. It's that simple. Over time, you will get chosen less often.

We logically know that each restaurant is its own "manufacturing" facility with the opportunity to surprise and delight or disappoint a customer each visit. Have you ever been to a sit-down restaurant and the food was a little off, or maybe the table service was a bit slow? You get the bill and ask yourself, was it worth it? You file that moment away and go about the rest of your day. It becomes a perception in your mind for the next time you are choosing where to dine.

THE GUEST PATH TO PURCHASE

Does this sound familiar at your house or among your friends?

"Where do you want to go eat?"

"I don't know. Where do you want to go?"

Someone tosses out a place to go. If your last experience with that place wasn't that great, you might say, "The last time we were there it wasn't that good, it wasn't worth it." And bam, it's vetoed! Just like that, that brand is off your list. That's the path to purchase that's informed by past experiences. Joy can be a differentiator in these consumer moments of choice.

What Do Guests Think of Us?
To drive traffic, we must win the debate to steal share

"What do you feel like?"
"I don't know, what do you want to eat?"

The "Moment of Choice"   The "Guest Experience"

What we are known for   Guest   Restaurant Experience
What describes our brand?   Path to   Satisfaction/Revisit
                             Purchase
Decision Barriers   Restaurant Frustrations
What limits frequency?   What can we improve?

As mentioned above, joy can be delivered uniquely within the four walls and even with delivery and take-out. If you are getting delivery or take-out, the value or making it "worth it" is more about the food and also the speed of service. Can you deliver joy in a delivery or take-out experience? Of course, but most businesses aren't really even contemplating this.

1. CONSUMER NEEDS DIDN'T FUNDAMENTALLY CHANGE

Since the emergence of Covid, there has been a lot of talk around the idea of "going back to normal." Another phrase we have been hearing concerns "the new normal." I honestly dislike both phrases, the second one in particular.

Convenience is a macro trend that has been around for decades. Covid only accelerated this movement in the restaurant industry, it didn't "create" it. When restaurants closed their dining rooms, consumers had no other choice than to access full service through curbside and delivery. Prior to Covid, they enjoyed dining in and occasionally did take-out. What we've learned is that eating at home remained a different "occasion" for consumers vs. dining in. As dining rooms reopened, the off-premises sales and traffic held steady as an incremental occasion.

2. CONVENIENT LOCATION IS A STATE OF MIND

In research, I often hear customers saying a restaurant or other business is not conveniently located. While there's some practical truth to that, it too often becomes a crutch. When consumers say it's "too far to drive" – that's the worst thing that you want to hear. It means that the experience is average, not memorable, making it not worth the drive. Every day, consumers drive past many options before pulling into the one where they ultimately dine. Convenient location is a state of mind. Think about your own behavior: do you drive to the first restaurant out of your neighborhood? Maybe sometimes, but most times you drive by quite a few before pulling into the final destination. How far will your customers drive for the experience?

3. RESISTING THE TEMPTATION TO TAKE MORE PRICE

"Taking price" - or increasing prices in non-industry language - is a necessary evil in any business, yet at the moment we are seeing 40-year high inflation and the industry is responding by taking unprecedented pricing action. When talking with countless leaders, the answer is often that they have to and don't have a choice, combined with the fact that competitors are taking price.

But now, the question is, when will consumers just opt out and stay home because it's not "worth it"? I would argue, we've already passed that point with 60% of consumers reporting they are cooking more at home because restaurant prices have gone up too much (November 2022). Guests are opting out because it's not worth it. The industry is getting ahead of itself taking menu pricing and doing less promotional pricing. Once menu prices are raised, you must "deal" them back.

Traffic is without a doubt a better indicator of brand health vs. inflated sales due to pricing action. We also know it's perfectly predictable that traffic goes down when you take price. After you lose the traffic, it never works to just lower the prices because typically you can't get back what you lost. Lower traffic plus lower checks mean you're dead in the water.

It's a vicious cycle, and in harsh terms, it goes something like this: You take price because costs are up, and traffic counts aren't enough to cover the cost increases. Yet, when you increase your price, logically you know some customers will opt out and not come back. Then, you resort to discounting your price to get customers back and your check average goes down. You have a ticket problem, and you're dead and the next regime will figure it out.

4. MAKING IT "WORTH IT"

Given that, shouldn't we be asking "what can we do to drive traffic through value instead of just raising prices to drive topline sales?"

As an industry, based on our consumer data, many restaurant experiences are on automatic pilot. Consumers tell us we herd them in and out like cattle instead of trying to engage with guests. Driving value is not about price but more about driving emotional connections to the brand. Again, I know we know this, but how can we keep increasing the price and delivering the same experience at best, and many times delivering a worse experience?

A paradigm shift must happen or the industry risks commoditization. It's a vicious doom loop. Without traffic, you lose sales. When you lose sales, you lose your best people because they aren't making enough money. Without great service, you lose more guests. Then repeat.

The good news is that there are brands that are doing it right by focusing on adding value and building brand loyalty. One example comes from my conversation with Khanh Nguyen, founder and CEO of ZaLat Pizza. The pizza delivery business is arguably one of the most competitive in the restaurant industry. It's easy to get caught up in pricing wars and discounting instead of adding value. When building ZaLat Pizza from the ground up, Khanh was creating value for his customers with his unique craveable pizza recipes. At times, they may cost more than the big brand pizza, so the ZaLat total experience has to be "worth it."

In the early days of Covid, Khanh and the ZaLat team had a different problem than full-service restaurants; his demand skyrocketed, driving massive trial of the brand. In fact, while the streets in Legacy West in Plano, Texas were silent and still, as Barry McGowan explained, Khanh chuckled that if you drove to Dallas, you would still see the emptiness on the streets until you turned the corner on Fitzhugh Avenue and saw the lines at ZaLat Pizza.

Given that the ZaLat business model relies heavily on third-party delivery drivers, that presented unique challenges for the brand, especially during unprecedented growth spikes. Khanh explained, "We spray-painted the entire parking lot with little crop circles that were six feet apart, and it was quite the sight to see all these Uber drivers standing in their little circles."

Thinking about all these Uber drivers standing in their little circles led Khanh to identify a brand gap that he turned into an opportunity to drive brand value and emotional connections. His aha moment – there was a missing brand connection when the pizza was delivered by the third-party driver. So, during Covid, he created the "pizza-gram" as part of his existing quality inspection process. He explained, "We have the Sharpie pen (used to mark the pizza as correct). So, I said, 'Hey, use the Sharpie pen and write a nice note inside the box to our customers to let them know that there's a person over here making this pizza, not some corporation.'" Now, that's a moment of added value joy, not only for the customer receiving the note, but for the employees as they write the notes.

The pizza-gram is a simple, no-cost value-add tactic that created a brand moment that guests appreciated. Khanh shared a customer story that stood out to him: "I remember one customer in particular. She got home and she opened up the pizza. She wrote us afterwards, and she said, 'I was having a really bad day, and your person could tell. They wrote me such a nice note inside this box. It really changed my mood and turn my day around.'" As I have mentioned before, restaurants deliver more than nourishment for our bodies; restaurants nourish our souls.

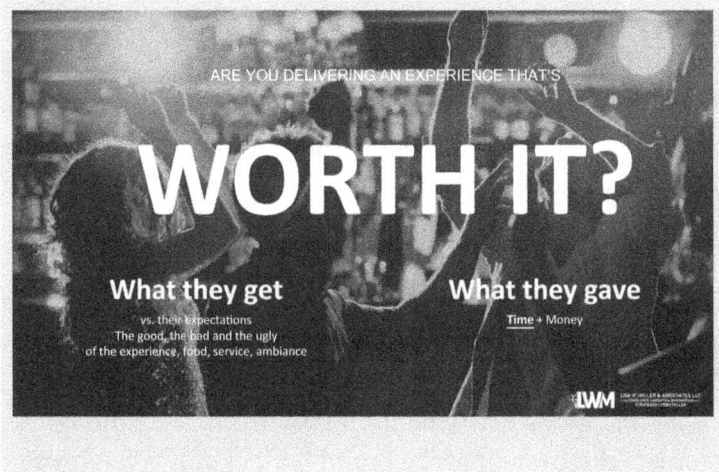

LESSONS LEARNED

1. DELIVER A JOYFUL EXPERIENCE AND WIN SHARE OF WALLET

I wanted to have a quick refresher on why joy matters to each of us personally, but importantly from a business perspective. Finding joy is a therapeutic way to overcome fear and anxiety. Joy is an emotion, not just a feeling. That moment in time that makes life worth living. That's joy. Joy isn't a destination but an attitude. Businesses capable of delivering joyful experiences earn customer loyalty and are more likely to weather the inevitable economic downturns. For businesses, it's all about making the experience "worth it" for their customers.

We need a reminder to resist temptation to just take price and not add value. Candidly, consumer data tells us that businesses are charging more and delivering the same or worse from an experience perspective. It's a slippery slope. Focus on delivering a joyful experience that's "worth it" and your customers will love your brand…. And the bonus: customers will be more forgiving when things inevitably go awry.

2.   TREAT EVERY DAY LIKE A GRAND OPENING

I would suggest that there has never been a more important time for brands. We have to deliver upon things we can't necessarily see or touch; it's how we make customers feel. The importance of brand is a concept that in all the performance marketing world, we've sort of left behind. We must remind consumers why they fell in love with brands in the first place or risk commoditization. Think of it like this. New store openings are exciting for a reason. Brand operators put their best foot forward when the doors open for the first time. There's a contagious excitement and joy in the air among the staff as customers discover what the brand is all about. What if you could replicate that feeling of joy each and every day? It's not why? But why not? You can and you must.

3.   MOVE FORWARD OR RISK FALLING BEHIND

There is no going back and there is no new normal, consumers are just moving forward as they always do. Covid just accelerated the movement in the restaurant industry. While the pandemic has impacted consumer behavior in ways that are here to stay, if a business stays static, it will ultimately fall behind.

Some businesses have been able to successfully pivot, others have not. If your business has been struggling to regain traffic, reassess the value equation and ask how you can deliver a more joyful experience.

THE GREAT REASSESSMENT – A GIFT FROM THE PANDEMIC

> *"Life is 10% what happens to us and 90% how we react to it."*
>
> – Dennis P. Kimbro

A S A SOCIETY, we tend to latch on to the negatives, the disasters, and the heartbreak, all without realizing what is on the other side. In the case of our Covid discussions, we have been discussing the differences between joy and fear.

So, how will the Covid-19 Pandemic be remembered five years from now or even 10 years from now? How will you remember it?

This is a question I think about all the time as I have been on my own journey interviewing consumers, frontline workers, and business leaders over the past couple of years. I have found that the answers from our collective memories demonstrate the dichotomy and tension we experienced. We were isolated from each other when we needed to be together. Through the tragedy and loss, there came inspiration, innovation, and growth. Through sorrow, we found appreciation. Joy was fleeting while some deeply emotional moments will never be forgotten.

1. THE EARLY DAYS SET THE STAGE

We have to think back to really understand when, how, and why this reassessment began. What inspired me to start tracking this reassessment trend was a conversation I had with a friend, Katrina Foster-Witherspoon, Head of Digital Operations, *D Magazine*, and an empty nester and single mom. She shared this story with me about her experiences from the very beginning of the pandemic: "When we heard that the world was coming apart, I called my two children (twenty-somethings – one in college, one working) and said, 'Pack a bag, I'm buying you a ticket home. This is where you have to be.' We didn't know what to expect with Covid. I told my kids, 'I have to have eyes on you.' The weeks turned into months of sharing a one-bedroom apartment because I was supposed to be an empty nester. The uncertainty was pretty terrifying."

She went on to tell me that even though she and her children were uncomfortably crammed into a small space, each of them had a chance to reflect and reassess. She said, "They finally had the breathing room in their lives, having room that would have never materialized had it not been for Covid." Both of her grown children ended up changing the trajectory of their lives, in a good way. Katrina believes Covid had turned out to be a "gift of time and reflection" as against what would have happened had they just stayed the course.

In talking with another friend — Rose Kaur, Managing Partner, Jester&Genius, A Brand Story Company — we discussed how Covid was a wake-up call of sorts for humanity, and how desperately we needed it. Rose's mother was taken by the virus halfway around the world in India. The tragedy of it all was that at the most important time when family was needed, she and her mother were away from each other. Rose reflected, "It makes you want to appreciate the people that matter; the things that matter, and the time that matters."

Rose continued, "I don't know what we are all racing towards, and what are we making our kids race towards? There's no pause. There's no breather for anyone." This race impacts our work life too. Rose shared her perspective on this: "The more you take time out for yourself and balance things out, the better things become at home and even at work. There's definitely a correlation."

2. GETTING TO THE HEART OF THE MATTER

> *"When people are willing to embrace the pause that Covid provided, they will be able to see what a gift it was."*
> – Sherri Landry EVP, CMO, CEC Entertainment

I fundamentally believe a gift from the pandemic will be a "Great Reassessment" and appreciation of what matters most to us. This can be a gift only IF we choose to hang on to it and keep it alive in our hearts, minds, and everyday lives.

During Covid, many consumers looked into their hearts and began to prioritize what was important. Consumers began focusing more on the things that gave them joy, or at least began making strides towards it. They pushed pause and began evaluating what mattered most at work and at home. This only became amplified as time marched on during the pandemic. Work-life balance was in the crossfire of this reassessment.

Did you pause at times to reflect, reassess, or reconsider things that were important in your life – whether in your personal life or professional roles?

Fast forward, as we rounded the two-year mark of Covid abruptly interrupting everyday lives, this consumer trend of reflecting and reassessing had been percolating under the surface. By December of 2022, half of Americans, 50% to be exact, reported they were seriously reconsidering and reassessing what was important in their life as a result of the pandemic. This was happening all the while companies had been shifting into overdrive, scrambling to stay afloat.

Consumers reported that it wasn't just about reassessing "how" they spent their time. They were reassessing "who" they spent time with. It was also where consumers chose to spend their money. Did they want to go out and do things or did they just want to stay home? We've already discussed how consumers were looking for experiences that were "worth it" at home, outside the home, and even at work. Consumers had been reevaluating everything and prioritizing what was important to them.

3. THE ISSUE: IT BECAME EASIER TO LEAVE THAN TO STAY

In early 2021, the headlines espoused the latest Covid trend about workers quitting in droves; a pundit somewhere was quick to call it "The Great Resignation." Then, there was the trending TikTok phrase called "Quiet Quitting." Do you remember that one? It's when workers weren't unhappy enough to quit, so they showed up for work only doing the bare minimum. The problem I have with these hype phrases is they only focus on the outcomes, what was going on at the moment, and not getting to the root causes.

So, under the surface, the driver of these catchphrases was actually something much bigger. It wasn't about resigning; it was about reassessing. Our research identified this theme and called it "The Great Reassessment." Our data supports it as the underlying deep emotion driving these headlines and the functional outcomes.

Consumers told us it was different. Resigning meant leaving a company, looking backward, while what they were really doing was reassessing what mattered most to them as they looked forward.

In looking at my data, this trend was perfectly predictable, yet most, including myself, didn't overtly pick it up until later. Why? We weren't using the right filter. The paradigm buster: workers at all levels were quitting their old jobs before they had a new job. That was considered blasphemy back in the day. Much has already been written about the stimulus checks, Covid pay, and the like, so we won't delve into too much detail here. Yet, in my interviews with industry leaders, I learned that it was not uncommon to have a frontline hourly worker tell a general manager that they were quitting because they could make more money staying home. It was especially challenging in the early days of reopening when sales were limited by seating capacity constraints suppressing the amount servers could earn.

But what was the role of work in their lives?

We talked earlier about the language of Covid, but there was (for many) a new language at home, too; "working from home" or WFH. There were Zoom meeting fails going viral and many got used to hearing, "You're on mute." There was "remote learning" with school-aged children and even college students back at home going to school. Combined, all of this made us reassess our lives.

4. WHY EMPLOYEE JOY MATTERS

> *"Culturally, what you really found out was who the a##hole bosses were and who weren't."*
> – Jack Gibbons, CEO, FB Society Restaurant Brands

Remember the customer backdrop for whether consumers choose your brand from the Value chapter. It's hard for your employees to deliver a joyful experience when they are exhausted. If they come across as frazzled with an "I don't want to be here" look, it will be hard to impress guests. Until field operators and franchisees can feel joyful, they're never going to be able to deliver joy to the guest. How can they?

Our data says that when looking for a job, the most important attributes are teamwork, culture, and managers having employees' backs. In fact, Kelli Valade told me about a location in which the entire kitchen staff was saying that they wanted to leave because they had been proactively approached by the restaurant across the street and offered $4 more per hour to lure them away. However, the head cook approached the general manager and expressed how much they all enjoyed working there and stated that they would all stay without asking for $4 per hour more, but meeting in the middle for $2 per hour more. There was clearly a level of comfort in the management to even have this conversation. Kelli explained, "Yes, it was about the money, but the good guys took care of their people and even protected them, and that made the difference."

ASK YOURSELF:

- *If your most valued employees were to be offered more money elsewhere, would they stay?*
- *What are the reasons beyond salary that they would want to stay?*
- *What makes your employee experience "worth it?"*

In today's tight labor market, creating a sense of belonging and a sense of family goes a long way in driving employee engagement and retention. Throwing more money at employees only goes so far. It doesn't create loyalty; it creates disloyalty to jump jobs more frequently. In this case, considering this was probably a 10% – 20% raise for most of the employees, their desire to stay speaks volumes to the culture of that organization.

Sherri Landry EVP, CMO, CEC Entertainment, shared her thoughts: "As leaders, you have to stay true to who you are. What we need right now is to have all managers help their people grow to their full potential. Companies that invest in the talent development process will succeed in the future." She went on to explain, "It's all about the people, kindness, and paying forward. Our team members are looking for a sense of belonging."

5. THE BOTTOM-LINE IMPACT

When it comes to driving traffic, nobody likes to get stuck in the discount wars. Relying too heavily on discounting is never a recipe for success. It creates promiscuous customer behavior as we train them to "wait for the next deal." The experience becomes commoditized, as we discussed in the Value chapter.

The same thing is happening when it comes to talent acquisition, but in reverse. Stick with me. We need to apply the same rigor to providing an employee experience that is "worth it" as we do for our guests. If we talk about salary alone, it will ultimately do the same things as heavy discounting – it doesn't build loyalty and people will jump to the next gig.

The value equation was and still is as important to employees as it is to consumers. When someone genuinely loves their job for whatever the reason, there is usually more to it than just money, as we just heard from Kelli Valade.

The value equation is the same: what they get vs. what they give. You'll notice "money" is the denominator too. Why? In today's market, your competitors may be willing to pay more, so why should your employee stay? Because "it's worth it!"

In talking with Jack Gibbons, CEO of FB Society, the pandemic opened up access to a talent pool nobody really talked about. There were so many furloughed people being laid off. Combined with the fact that some companies handled those layoffs poorly, it presented unprecedented access to talent. Jack explained, While everyone else was zigging, we were definitely zagging. We wouldn't have the team we have today had it not been for the crisis."

So, the restaurant industry hasn't always been the best employer – finding the right balance from compensation and work-life balance perspectives. Anita Adams, CEO of Black Bear Diner, explained, "I've always thought a lot about that, and now, we have the ability to really make an impact on that." When you worked in the office every day from seven in the morning to six o'clock at night, or later, it doesn't give much space when you have to take care of personal matters. She continued, "Life just happened after five. I've even reflected when we shuttered our offices, it was a very tough transition as my personal and professional life had never blended like that before. But I realized it's powerful and can be a very good thing."

When it came to talent acquisition, she shared, "You should be talking about people in a way that's not about just filling out rosters and throwing out compliments. You should talk about it in the context of how we care for people, how we pay them exactly what they need to make and more; we give them all the benefits they need, but we also give them this notion of giving them space to let their life just happen."

LESSONS LEARNED

1. UNDERSTAND YOUR EMPLOYEES AS DEEPLY AS YOUR CUSTOMERS

To win the talent wars, businesses must apply the same rigor to learning about employees' needs as they do their customers'. That investment will yield dividends.

It's the need for joy and socialization; the need for each other; that compassion and kindness for each other. These insights don't stop at the office. If you were an office worker, hospital worker, or hourly worker of any kind, you showed up to work, did the job, and that was that. With labor shortages, the transition of power shifted during Covid. Previously, companies had been in the driver's seat vs. the employees. That's no longer the case. And honestly, for our country, I believe this is a good thing. It's painful at the moment because the scales have flipped so dramatically, but it will settle down with time.

Why It Matters: We can't simply transact with employees on salaries.

In our customer experience, we don't want the conversation to be just about price. So why are we letting the employee experience become so much about salary only? Your answer better not be "because that's what everyone else is doing and it's the only way to compete."

Is it? That approach is the "race to nowhere."

2. REFRAME 'RETENTION'

Why do so many obsess about "turnover" which is the metric we don't want to increase? Instead, shouldn't we be obsessing about improving what we want to increase - which is "retention?" That got me thinking, is there a better word than "retention" that could be more positive? I honestly hadn't thought much about it before until I looked up synonyms for retention – Containment, Control, Detainment,

Detention, Holding, and Reserving. The antonyms for retention are Freedom and Liberation.

I would encourage you to create space/time for workers to dip their toe into something that they have always wanted to try. Maybe a finance person wants to learn about social media. Maybe a data analytics person wants to play around in a big data set. Find your joy at work and make space (time and resources) for your team to find their joy.

UNINTENDED CONSEQUENCES

*"There is no greater hell than
to be a prisoner of fear."*

– Theodore Roosevelt

DURING MY INTERVIEWS, CEOs told me that the pandemic seemed like a lifetime ago and that they have moved on. Consumers concur, with over two-thirds of Americans agreeing that we have to move beyond Covid and get back to living our lives. I wholeheartedly believe that this is a good thing – a *great* thing, in fact.

Yet, as you might imagine, I still have lingering questions that need answering:

- What about the third of Americans who haven't or can't move on beyond Covid?
- How has the pandemic impacted consumers' ability to trust?
- How will the pandemic be remembered five years from now or even 10 years from now? Will it be more about the many positive outcomes, or will it be more about the negative outcomes?

1. DEALING WITH THE AFTERMATH

It's perfectly predictable that our memories of Covid and the pandemic will fade over time. The positive outcomes of Covid will likely be amplified and stand the test of time, while the more negative memories will fade. Why is that? Did you know that there is research that shows that our negative memories fade more quickly? It's how we as humans cope and deal with negative stressors, and it helps us be more resilient and optimistic. Fascinating, right?[9] It's like a real-world version of the neuralyzer in the movie *Men in Black* – the device that with a flash of a bright light, boom, the memories are gone.

But before those memories fade, I feel that it's critical to address some of the negative unintended consequences head-on before too much time passes, lest we forget, and the important lessons learned will be lost forever.

Think of it like this: when it rains too much, we watch helplessly as the water rises, creating devastating floods. Yet, we know that it is not until the water recedes that we can really see the damage done. It's the same during the pandemic. We watched and lived through the ups and downs of the pandemic, yet the long-term impact of the decisions made over the two-and-a-half-year period is still being revealed. I firmly believe that we won't even understand the full impact for years to come.

And, just like rebuilding happens after a flood, the same holds true today as we continue the rebuilding process after the devastation of Covid. We are rebuilding our economy and, honestly, we are still rebuilding ourselves.

I do want to say that none of this is a political statement.

---

[9] See "Why good memories are less likely to fade."
https://www.bbc.com/news/health-27193607.

We have had two different administrations at the helm during the pandemic and it could be argued neither really shined nor showed more confidence than the other. I don't have any conspiracy theories about anything, but I do have mountains of data to speak to the implications of decisions on the average consumer. I recognize that everyone's point of view is different, so if you think any of these is actually a positive, that's OK!

2. AMPLIFIED FEAR, ISOLATION, AND LONELINESS

There is an undercurrent of lingering anxiety that is now permanently part of our psyche and our culture.

In our minds, as we were told to stay home, we remembered and craved the experiences that were taken away. The isolation from our friends, family, and co-workers at first seemed like a nice respite from the world but eventually turned into pandemic fatigue.

Sadly, Covid has permanently changed many of us in that we have become more "anxious" than before the pandemic. What does that mean? It means that many Americans still filter everything through a lens of increased anxiety. Over one-third of Americans (36%) believe that Covid permanently changed them to be more anxious. We know that how you experienced Covid varied dramatically by gender, age, and ethnicity. So, it shouldn't be surprising that when digging deeper into this data by cohort, there are significant differences.

% Agree/Strongly Agree: I am concerned that Covid has permanently made me more anxious than I was before the pandemic.

- **36% Total US, Americans 18+ years old (November 2022)**

- 49% Moms with kids under 18 vs Dads 37%

- 47% Gen Z (18 – 24-year-olds) vs. 34% Boomers (55 – 73 years old)

- 46% Asian vs. 45% Hispanic vs. 31% Caucasian

First, about half of moms with kids under 18 report being more anxious and changed by Covid, which is significantly more than dads, coming in at about just over a third. Throughout the pandemic, moms have been more fearful and slower to venture out to re-enter the activities outside the home. Call it maternal "mama bear" instinct.

Moms, particularly with children under 12 years old, carried a significant burden during the pandemic, having to navigate closed daycares and remote schooling, on top of a likely change in their own work situation. Some moms had to quit their jobs to take care of their family. Moms are the unsung heroes of the pandemic, yet unfortunately, it comes at a cost. When moms are anxious, that can clearly have an impact on their children for years to come.

Why does this matter? Women drive 85% of purchase decisions. (Forbes 2019) So one could argue that as goes women's sentiments and behaviors, so goes the economic recovery.

Gen Z, 18- to 24-year-olds, were also hit hard by the pandemic. The Covid lockdowns started right at Spring Break. This generation was in high school or college at the start of the pandemic. For high schoolers, stripped away were the typical milestones of high school sports, proms, graduations, and more. One college student shared with me, "The lockdown happened during Spring Break. We weren't allowed to go back to the campus. The school hired a moving company, threw our stuff in boxes, and shipped it back to our homes. I haven't been back since." Important life lessons, experiences of "adulting" and living on their own didn't happen as campuses across the country closed. The isolation of these formidable years took a toll. Today, Gen Z is the loneliest generation in the country with 32% stating they are lonely vs. 23% for the Total US. They are also *least* likely to agree that we need to get beyond Covid and back to normal lives (53% vs 69% Total US). Shocking, right?! Most might think that they are young and carefree. Covid changed that for many Gen Z's.

Hispanics and Asian consumers also have lingering fear and anxiety. Asian consumers are more likely to be fearful about the virus itself. They are most likely to continue wearing masks and having a desire to continue to get booster shots to protect them against the virus. By pulling back on their activities outside the home, Asian consumers are much more likely to say they have saved money during the pandemic. The impact on Hispanic consumers is completely different in that their anxieties are more financially related. Hispanics are significantly more likely to be living paycheck to paycheck and concerned that they will not have money to live comfortably in the future.

Rising violence is instilling fear and having a negative impact on the economy

I introduced the concept of bad customer behavior in the chapter "The Customer Isn't Always Right." These bad behaviors have continued to escalate, so much so that many Americans have become fearful of venturing out in public. Fear of personal safety is higher than fear of Covid. The nationally publicized shootings and crowd surges that we all have seen drive consumer comments such as these:

- *"When I go to the movies now, I make sure I sit close to an exit door" – a Gen Z female*
- *"When I go to a concert, my friends and I talk about active shooters and crowd surges, and make sure we have a plan if something happens" – a Gen X Male*

It's not just these national stories, it's the daily local stories and the brazen nature of the crimes that is disturbing and making many Americans fearful of going out. Being prepared for violence can save your life, yet the fact that these plans are needed is negatively impacting sales and traffic across the country. Moms, Hispanics, and Blacks are most likely to be pulling back their behavior.

> **% Agree/Strongly Agree: I am more fearful today than before the pandemic to be out in public not because of Covid, but due to bad behavior and rising violence**
>
> • **42% Total US, Americans 18+ years old**
>
> • 54% Hispanics
>
> • 52% Moms
>
> • 49% Blacks

New York City Riots – Photo courtesy of John Eales

3. COMPELLED TO TAKE SIDES – SOCIAL CIRCLES SHRANK

It takes a long time to build trust but only a fleeting moment for it to erode. In the early days, consumers looked to the government and science for ways to stay safe and protect those around us but as time went on, they began losing faith.

As quickly as mandates and solutions were put in place to protect us, there was often new information indicating otherwise or at minimum making us second-guess ourselves and the powers that be. It was exhausting.

Choices made in response to the economic crisis eroded trust for millions of people. For those who were skeptical by nature, doubt and trepidation increased in response to the constantly conflicting data. It will take time to rebuild trust in the government and trust in the science for a significant number of Americans.

% Agree/Strongly Agree (November 2022)

TOTAL US

- *55% I've lost trust in the government to do what's best for the people*

- *43% I am losing trust in the experts' ability to understand and predict Covid*

While businesses and communities tried to come together to move forward, government decisions and leadership divided us. The longer we stayed in lockdown mode, the more something changed. We were not only fearful of the virus, but we also became fearful of each other.

If you are a business leader, take that hat off for a minute. As a consumer, did you have any awkward feelings when you first ventured out and were surrounded by people you didn't know? Maybe in the back of your mind, you were thinking about the fact that you didn't know who had been exposed to whom.

By December 2020, the trending memes of the day were about making plans but hoping the other person would cancel first. "Just staying home" was the sentiment that was now ingrained. It became comical to have these true (or maybe not-so-true) reasons we continued to "stay home," hunkering down in isolation in our own little bubbles away from other humans.

As the isolation and fear continued to grow, it ended up being contentious and divisive. Unfortunately, and unintentionally, Americans seemed compelled to take sides on the various Covid mandates and regulations.

Think of it this way, we wanted to get back out there, but we also wanted to be totally protected. It was a bit of "stay away from me" and "wear a mask" mentality. And if you had a different opinion about vaccines or masks, public culture deemed you as a "bad person" for your beliefs. For those who were in the minority, it simply made them dig their heels in more. A recipe for a divided nation.

ASK YOURSELF:

During the pandemic, did you find yourself pulling back on who you spent your time with? If yes, you were not alone. Some of you reading this might have agreed with that, while the others may not understand at all.

Point made! Consumer sentiment is still highly divided. Taking sides was inevitable.

By March of 2021, as the political and cultural stressors beyond just Covid grew larger, consumers' social circles became smaller and smaller. What happened? Instead of discussing these differences and seeking to understand each other, our data showed that consumers decided that it was easier to just step away from those with whom they disagreed. In fact, close to four in 10 basically "unfriended" someone, spending less time and energy with friends and family members who had different cultural or political views. A tragedy for our country.

- *38% of Americans reported spending less time and energy with friends, extended family and acquaintances based on their cultural and political views, not just due to Covid. (March 2021)*

4. INEQUALITIES GREW

The longer the lockdown lasted, the more the many inequalities grew and highlighted differences in how we not only viewed the pandemic but how we experienced it. Existing gaps grew painfully larger across so many parts of Americans' lives – from access to healthcare, social justice issues, basic Wi-Fi, and even basic necessities as the food supply chain issues escalated across the country.

As we awkwardly fumbled our way through 2020, the tension was bubbling and mounting under the surface. All of these issues contributed to the perfect storm crashing down on business in the spring and summer of 2021.

5. ENOUGH IS ENOUGH – UNENGAGED AND TUNING OUT

I'm not a media industry expert by any stroke, but if you compare viewership declines to sales and traffic, it would be clear that the news media industry fired many of their customers during Covid.

In the first year of the pandemic, Americans craved information to keep them safe, with a required healthy dose of hope, optimism, and joy. What we got instead were disturbing and relentless images of people on ventilators and morgues overflowing with body bags. A typical two-week news cycle turned into two-plus years. It was more than most of us could take.

The inundation of news stories about deaths and infection rates made us more anxious. Yet, much like a car wreck, we could not look away and continued tuning in, at least for a while. While I do have a new appreciation of the work it takes to create content that resonates, our data shows that the media contributed to the rising anxiety during the peak of the pandemic. By mid-2022, Americans were telling the news outlets that they had enough as news media viewership plummeted.[10]

[10] Neal Rothschild and Sara Fischer, "News Engagement Plummets as Americans Tune Out," Axios, July 12, 2022, https://www.axios.com/2022/07/12/news-media-readership-ratings-2022.

> *% Agree/Strongly Agree (November 2022)*
>
> TOTAL US
>
> - *56% I don't trust the media to report just the facts of the news*
> - *36% I have stopped watching the news because it's so depressing*
> - *37% I have stopped watching the news because it's so biased*

The implication is that consumers are still hungry to learn and stay informed without the hype or overkill. The news media will have to innovate to regain consumer trust and their viewership, especially in the midst of continued fragmentation of news options.

6. THE "ESSENTIAL" BUSINESS OF RESTAURANTS

When the restaurant industry was deemed "non-essential" it created a monumental shift in its trajectory. There will be much debate about what really was "essential" vs. "non-essential" to protect us from the virus, yet the research shows that human connections are indeed "essential."

For restaurants, the loss of revenue for businesses was just the tip of the iceberg. The unintended consequence of the shutdown impacted jobs and livelihoods. Restaurant jobs are valuable, and without them, being honest, nobody else (including the government) can make up for the difference. As Barry McGowan, CEO of Fogo de Chão recalled, "The people our industry employs, I would say is the first rung of employment. It's the first job at times, and sometimes it's that important second job for extra income, or even it's that transitional job." He continued, "Every community in today's America should realize the value we add, the people we employ, the joy we deliver. And the convenience we offer. And I'll say this: without it, communities are pretty scary."

LESSONS LEARNED

1. CHOOSE WORDS WISELY WHEN IN CRISIS MODE

I don't claim to have the answers for the public policy issues, yet the data speaks volumes and should inform future planning policy discussions and communication strategies.

There must be a better way that protects yet avoids creating permanent fear and anxiety. There was wartime language, the kind used when fighting against an enemy, and if you don't win, you die. Americans responded to the call to action. It turns out that this lingering fear and anxiety are not good for many Americans' mental health and hasn't been good for the economy either.

2. OVERCOMING THE NEGATIVE IMPACTS WILL TAKE TIME

As the "Covid flood waters" have begun to recede, we are just beginning to see the hidden damage under the surface. The unintended consequence of all of this is that as a country, broadly speaking, we are more divided, and our social skills and conflict resolution skills leave something to be desired. No doubt, working from home also contributed to these issues. These and many more experiences fundamentally changed us, and the data shows that for some Americans, Covid changed them permanently for the worse.

I am not trying to be overly dramatic, yet I wonder if there is ultimately a comparison to the Silent Generation which carried forward attitudes and behaviors learned during the Great Depression. These aren't things that are consciously carried forward, more just ingrained based on experiences that you live through. Time will tell.

3. CHECK IN WITH YOUR TEAMS – ARE THEY OK? ARE THEY PREPARED?

As a business leader, what does this mean to you?

- Know that one out of four of your employees is likely feeling some anxiousness that they may or may not be talking about. Ask if they are OK.
- Make sure that your frontline managers and employees know the plan if something does go wrong. I assume that most have a plan, but is it well cascaded down the chain?

RECONNECTING
WITH AMERICA

"America was hungry to dine out. But more importantly, hungry to reconnect."

– John Cywinski

T HE PANDEMIC TAUGHT us many lessons. Some were applicable to society as a whole and others varied based on region, industry, demography, and a host of other variables. It is clear from my research that one of the most common threads among everyone was the realization that there is more than one way to solve a challenge. Resourcefulness was on full display as the pandemic endured and those who got better at finding creative ways to handle challenges fared better in the long run.

Since these waters were completely uncharted, the prior strategy of looking at what your competition was doing in search of insights or comparisons did not serve anyone well. The real focus had to be on applying "out-of-the-box" thinking with a focus on what the consumer wanted at a time when the tension between fear versus joy of going out was still high. In order for economic recovery to truly begin, it was up to brands to reconnect with America showing them that joy could be greater than fear. The emotional desire for connecting with others outside of our home ultimately prevailed, although admittedly it has taken longer than anyone would have hoped for.

PULLING CONSUMERS FORWARD

Consumer decisions to go back out or not were made at a very personal level. Successful brands were able to listen to what consumers wanted and needed to feel safe, then go a step further to not only provide those things but make sure the joy was still present in the experience. A part of this was taking a good look inside and ensuring you were clear on your brand strengths and brand identity. When facing adversity, leaning into these strengths kept brands from losing their identity and able to continue providing the needed brand differentiation and the level of service customers had come to know and expect.

Telling the larger brand story is not just about focusing on the food being promoted that month or showing the obligatory gatherings of having fun. It needed to be much bigger than that. It literally was pulling the consumer forward to give them reasons to get up off their sofas to find joy outside their homes. Brands had to move from the transactional nature of performance and retail marketing tactics to deeper, more emotional connections of why they fell in love with a brand in the first place.

In the midst of a global pandemic, brand leaders faced new challenges of how best to invite customers back. Many brands created advertising campaigns designed to lean into the segment of the population craving the experiences they had lost. There was a nostalgia for what felt like days long since gone when people could meet out in public and share a human connection.

John Cywinski shared this key insight with me, "What was missing during the pandemic was getting out of your home, to just drive around the corner to your neighborhood place to sit down and have a drink or a steak to just connect. It's all those little life moments." He continued, "It could be about a child going off to college, it could be about a child getting married, it could be about a relationship issue or a financial matter. But they take place in these little tables and booths over a meal. The meal is just there to facilitate the interaction." One of Applebee's more creative campaigns leaned into reboots of the classic television sitcom *Cheers,* complete with the theme song. In case you don't remember, it went a little something like this: "Sometimes you want to go where everybody knows your name… and they're always glad you came…." The commercial was then poetically tied together with, "Welcome back, America…. It sure is good to see you…."

Anita Adams reinforced just how important it was for a brand to have a strong sense of self-awareness and the conviction to stick to it. "It can all be overwhelming when you look at it globally, but I think we just kept looking inside to recognize why guests loved us. We've got a great team and we just need to stay true to who we are and not morph and become something we're not. And I think certain brands have made decisions for reasons that were important to them. But we've taken a position to say we actually are just going to protect who we are."

Even the National Restaurant Association was doing its part to invite consumers back to dining rooms across America. In August 2020, in collaboration with many partners, the industry association launched a restaurant revival television campaign called, "The Sounds We Crave."[11] The television spot featured one-of-a-kind unique sensory experiences of dining out to rekindle the emotional connection that could be found only in restaurant dining rooms across America and not from a take-out box.

---

[11] National Restaurant Association. "National Restaurant Association – The Sounds We Crave :30," August 30, 2020. https://www.youtube.com/watch?v=Bnn_AWX-qU8.

THE BACKLASH - WAS IT TOO SOON?

As with the polarization of consumer sentiment throughout the pandemic, it was perfectly predictable that there would be discourse about brands advertising and inviting guests back. As you might imagine, I tracked consumer sentiment around this delicate balance of re-opening the country vs. public health. In July 2020, the country was leaning into the position that businesses couldn't survive another lockdown by a slim margin. Yet just two short months later in September 2020, the vast majority of consumers were on board with reopening the economy.

	July 2020	September 2020	Pt. Chg.
Businesses will not survive if the country moves back to another full shutdown. The solution is a balance between safety protocols and personal choice to go out or not even if cases continue to accelerate	55%	68%	+13
Shut it down now. The pandemic is out of control, we must go back to full shut down to protect ourselves and contain the spread even if it means businesses suffer.	45%	32%	-13

As leaders scrambled to find ways to reconnect with their customers, the divisive regulations and consumer sentiment sometimes made it feel like a no-win situation. There were pundits suggesting it was 'too soon' and some went so far as to say 'irresponsible' for brands to be persuading guests via advertising to come back to dine-in at restaurants. Backlash mounted on social media and in the court of public opinion, even though two-thirds of all Americans were ready to get back out into the world. Much like there was more than one way to solve any problem, there would be more than one strategy for appealing to your ideal customer – the ones who wanted to come back. Businesses could not sit back and alienate those who wanted to venture out and spend money; in fact, it was quite the opposite. They had to stand firm on the journey to not only service the customers coming back, but also to entice those still sitting on the fence and at home comfortably on their sofas.

In his conversations with me, John Cywinski was very candid about his experiences during this period of re-engagement. It was clear there were some brands that felt the right answer was to wait it out, sit on the sidelines, and not advertise. He did not look at this as a negative in any way, since he was aware re-engaging with the public carried a risk. Any misstep at a time where everything was being scrutinized would undoubtedly bring more pressure than anyone wanted to deal with. He and his team felt confident in their ability to connect with authenticity, which meant not forcing anyone into a particular channel of business but instead reinforcing their mission to be there however they were needed.

THE SPARK: RECONNECTIONS BETWEEN STAFF AND THE REGULARS

No matter what your opinion is on how we got to the point where these commercials could even be considered divisive or how individual companies took matters into their own hands, there are many stories from the frontlines of how life in the restaurant industry started returning to normal. December 2021 showcased strong holiday sales despite a resurgence in Covid cases with numbers spiking into January. Many people still had not ventured out but the bartenders and servers we spoke to recounted how excited they were to start seeing their *regulars* back in the restaurant. Whether it was the marketing or the pent-up demand, something had shifted enough for a significant number of people to start re-engaging with each other and the world as a whole.

This shouldn't be so surprising, though. Deciding you are ready to finally get out of the house and eat out is not an epic decision like planning a trip to Disney World, where you have to check calendars, book flights and hotels, and probably spend an arm and a leg. What was missing during the pandemic was hopping in your car on a whim and driving around the corner to your favorite restaurant just to get out of the house, celebrate the success of a relative, or mourn the loss of a loved one. These tables and booths were sites of more than a meal; they were the places facilitating the interactions, and the leaders recognized this.

It might appear from everything presented thus far that the re-entry of consumers into the post-Covid world had more to do with personal preference than anything else. But in reality, reconnecting with Americans looked different from the brand perspective as well. Small chains with 62 restaurants and larger national chains with thousands of stores had to adapt in their own ways. There were common table stakes like offering outdoor seating, delivery, and to-go options, but that is where the similarities ended. Sometimes being a larger establishment was actually a handicap because of the perceived fear from consumers about interacting with larger crowds, thus increasing exposure risks. Yet, on the contrary, the larger companies had more resources and options to work with in an effort to meet changing consumer demands.

There was no right or wrong answer in the moment, and each CEO made quick and decisive decisions based on the information available to them at a given point in time. So many factors went into these strategies that none of us could look back and second-guess the reason at the moment. John Cywinski focused heavily on the nostalgia marketing we mentioned earlier, but with over 1,600 restaurants in his network, he also cut the menu options by roughly 35% to streamline supply ordering and minimize potential waste. While Cywinski was doing that, Barry McGowan leveraged his smaller network to focus on exceptional service levels and adding more options to the experience and menu. Both were successful in their own rights because of the focus on their respective core businesses and leaning into what had always made their brands special.

BOTTOM LINE - REASSURING WITH SAFETY STILL MATTERS

What did look the same for CEOs, from companies of all sizes, was the need to comply with new and changing mandates. Leaders spoke specifically to the health and safety protocols by which everyone needed to abide. There was some debate as to whether the protective measures would be shared equally by all members of the frontline team or if a dedicated position would be created. No one had ever heard of a sanitation specialist before, but for many leaders, that seemed like the safer way to go. One person per shift would be responsible to literally walk through the restaurant and sanitize everything: every surface, tabletop, chair, and doorknob. The result would hopefully not only be reduced infections, but also a more relaxed experience for patrons who could see the visual cues of what was being done for their safety.

LESSONS LEARNED

1. CHANGE THE PARADIGM: CUSTOMERS ARE NOT COMING BACK

There's no going back, only forward to create "re-trial". Brands need to remind consumers why they fell in love with their brands in the first place so that consumers get up off of their sofas and through their doors. Going out has become the "new behavior" after consumers have stayed home for over two years.

There is no more important time for brands than now. In the competitive sea of sameness, brand differentiation should be the top priority for every brand to win customer hearts, loyalty and share of wallet. Yet, it can be challenging to dedicate the necessary time and energy to masterfully develop it and keep it relevant. I've been there. It's easy to get sucked into the daily grind of driving sales and traffic today and over time, the brand essence becomes diluted and often lost. We think we are building the brand, but it's hard to do that in a fifteen-second commercial promoting the next new product launch of value limited time only offer.

2. LEAD WITH YOUR STRENGTHS, DON'T CHASE COMPETITORS

Brands that emerged stronger on the other side of the pandemic used the opportunity to sharpen the core of the brand proposition. When adversity hits, brands should lead with their strengths, don't try to be something you are not. Those that strayed too far from their core to survive often ended up losing their brand identities along the way.

Brands should absolutely be "tracking" competitors, yet there's a difference between tracking and chasing them. Brands that aren't clear on what they stand for can be led off course by chasing competitors' menus, pricing, and promotional strategies. It happens more often than you might think leading to that sea of sameness and lack of brand differentiation.

3. 3. GET COMFORTABLE WITH BEING UNCOMFORTABLE

Just like we discussed in the "Accelerated Innovation" chapter, reconnecting with America required leaders to step out of their comfort zone. There were risks no matter how you looked at it. Doing nothing and sitting it out was not an option for the leaders that I spoke to. Most decisions invited the court of public opinion to weigh in whether it be the news media, pundits, or consumers. Brands that leaned into marketing and customer experiences early in the re-opening months fared better than those that waited on the sidelines.

THE BUSINESS OF JOY CONTINUES

"Chance favors the prepared mind."

– Louis Pasteur

F IRST, I HADN'T intended to end with 13 chapters in this book. It's a bit ominous. Yet, it was on Friday the 13th of March 2020 that this journey officially began with the declaration of a national emergency, so I decided to run with it.

After working on this book for months, it's 2:00 a.m., and I'm literally struggling with this last chapter. There are so many important lessons spinning through my head, from the story of Katrina, a single mom who just needed to have "eyes on her grown kids" during the pandemic, bringing them home to shelter in place with her – a situation that changed the trajectory of her children's lives for the better. To Jack Gibbons, who decisively ran "into the pandemic instead of away from it," leading FB Society Restaurants to come out of Covid stronger on the other side. And, from Margo Manning at Dave & Busters having to "prepare to be closed indefinitely" for the first time in her career. To Fogo de Chão's Barry McGowan completely embracing "leading with joy and reassuring with safety."

While our individual Covid stories and experiences were certainly different, as you have read throughout the book, the common thread is that all of us *lived it*. That is exactly what makes this book different than most other historical reflections.

But what's the "So what? Now what?" from all of this? *We got to the other side.*

Next time, it may not be called Covid, yet as a leader, you've got to be ready for whatever <u>it</u> is. It wasn't chance and it wasn't luck – it was survival mode, innovation, and decisive leadership that got businesses to the other side of the pandemic. We have to remember to not let ourselves get complacent.

It was hard work to get through a global pandemic, and we know that not everybody did get through it. A lot of businesses failed – some because they didn't have the critical mass, others because they didn't have the financial means to weather the storm, and still some that just didn't pivot quickly enough to survive.

I've captured what I believe are the most important lessons learned to carry forward as it relates to your customers, your brand, and your employees. Under each, I pose a question for you to ponder. I encourage you to really think about it so you can learn and take action.

They are organized by one of four unifying concepts:

1. <u>Changing the paradigms</u> – The pandemic jolted many businesses out of autopilot, challenging conventional wisdoms. These may seem nuanced, but they are monumentally important as businesses move beyond the pandemic with post-pandemic strategies.
2. <u>Flipping the switch</u> – To keep the lights "on", the switch was flipped into supersonic mode and great things happened. The pandemic enabled creative and accelerated problem-solving as we have never seen before. No one wants a repeat of the

pandemic yet keeping that sense of urgency and focus is necessary moving forward.

3. <u>Perspective matters</u> – Covid took a lot from us, yet if we look beyond the tragedy, we can look back and take to heart some of the things we should never repeat, and hold close those things that made us stronger.

4. <u>Joy is a journey, not a destination</u> – Thankfully, the Covid pandemic is moving into our memories, yet finding joy remains journey not a destination, as there will always be new challenges to face. We will end where we began with why joy is critical to us individually, and as importantly how brands can succeed by delivering joy to employees and customers.

CHANGING THE PARADIGMS.

1. CUSTOMERS ARE 'NEVER COMING BACK'

How are you going to re-introduce your brand - reframing as "trial"?

Think about it this way: customers are "never coming back"; they are always moving forward. As the saying goes, if your brand is standing still, you are falling behind. If you were launching your brand for the first time, you would explain to prospective customers what your brand stands for, why they should come. It's driving awareness and trial.

Covid created a gap in the normal conversion funnel. As you market to your customers, think about it as "re-trial", not just coming "back." Why not make every day feel like a grand opening for your employees and your customers? This one little nuance will impact everything you do, from menu development to operations and marketing.

I would suggest that there has never been a more important time for brands than now. Unlocking the pent-up demand has been a challenge, to say the least. Many consumers may have forgotten about what your brand stands for after staying home during Covid. With inflation driving price increases and then brands dealing them back down, we risk commoditizing our brands with too many value promotions and discounts. It's paramount to re-engage and connect with customers to drive brand love and brand differentiation.

2. THE CUSTOMER ISN'T ALWAYS RIGHT

How are you adding joy and value to your employee experience?

Today it's easier to leave than it is to stay, and that, my friends, is what needs to change. Your employees are your brand ambassadors; they make the magic happen each and every day at the hundreds of thousands of restaurants around the country. It doesn't stop at the unit level: your regionals, district managers, and restaurant support staff all enable success.

When it comes to driving traffic, nobody likes to get stuck in the discount wars, as we discussed earlier. Relying too heavily on discounting is never a recipe for success. It creates promiscuous customer behavior as we train customers to "wait for the next deal." The same thing is happening when it comes to talent acquisition but in reverse. Instead of discounting, companies are throwing insane amounts of money at people. That will create that same unwanted behavior – no loyalty, no belonging, just "waiting for the highest offer."

As an industry, we need to do better. Just like we talked about reminding your customers why they fell in love with your brand, we need to remind potential employees how great this industry is. The upcoming generation doesn't have a favorable opinion of working in the restaurant industry – because "it's not worth it."

We have to focus resources on understanding the hopes, wants, and dreams of our employees to the same extent that we do for our customers. This is the time for the Chief People Officers and HR professionals to shine. My experience is that those training dollars are often some of the first to get cut.

Those who truly invest in these more strategic employee studies will be leaps and bounds ahead of those who don't. Your people are your secret sauce.

FLIPPING THE SWITCH.

3. INNOVATION AT SCALE

How will you create more space and focus for accelerated innovation to continue?

When it was time to innovate or die, the industry created herculean innovations in record time. Yet I fear we have already lapsed back to our old ways. I recently saw a restaurant publication article noting that the industry's menu pipeline was lackluster and quite empty. We've lost that sense of urgency.

Most companies believe that they have a culture of innovation. The reality is, they don't.

As leaders, you have to make space for innovation. You may have had conversations with your team to ask why they can't replicate that speed or creativity. As we've gotten back to the daily "running of the business," innovation has fallen to the side.

Those companies that harness the learning from accelerated innovation will leap ahead of competitors.

4. HIGH TECH VERSUS HIGH TOUCH

How will you balance technology-enabled solutions without stripping away the joy?

The concept of reducing consumer friction and adding people where value is added is 'understood', yet how this comes to fruition is still a work in progress. We have to ponder why there was friction in the

THE BUSINESS OF JOY CONTINUES

first place. Is it possible that the consumer frustration was coming from not having enough well-trained people?

Accelerated technology innovation is a great thing, don't get me wrong. Yet, I do worry that too much technology could erode brand differentiation and unintentionally create even more commoditization of hospitality experiences. We got a peek at what it would be like to stay home, be isolated and be deprived of many joyful activities outside our homes. We made it work, yet hospitality by definition should be a people business. Without the people, restaurants become merely another food transaction instead of a brand experience.

PERSPECTIVE MATTERS.

5. LISTEN FOR WHAT YOU DON'T WANT TO HEAR

How will you encourage more productive yet sometimes uncomfortable debate and discussion to get to better ideas?

Somewhere along the way, having a different opinion became negatively amplified during the pandemic. It is just sad that the pandemic created this even greater divide. If you did anything, the other side would attack you. Growing up in the South, there's this saying, "No matter how flat you make the pancake, there are always two sides." No right or wrong, just two sides.

We are still unwinding the outcomes of this divide. Our data shows that consumers retreated from those with differing opinions as they felt it was simply too exhausting to listen and debate them. How tragic! That isolation from difficult conversations eroded social skills, leading to, in my humble opinion, the very bad customer behavior we have seen.

From a business perspective and in life, it's important to be open to differing opinions. Getting only positive reinforcement is a sure recipe for disaster. I tell my clients when it comes to doing brand research, sometimes the consumer will tell you that your baby (the brand) is ugly. Clients cringe when they hear that, yet they know that's how brands get stronger, stay relevant, and stand the test of time.

It's OK to disagree with one another. When I'm doing focus groups with consumers, I tell them, if we are always agreeing with each other, someone isn't speaking up and saying what's really on their minds. That's what happens in work meetings.

It's uncomfortable to disagree with someone, but sometimes we seek just to be seen and heard. Be open when someone chimes in with a contrarian view.

- Listen to it
- Consider it
- Debate it

Covid taught us that ideas get better, not worse, when you debate them. You find solutions that might not have been on the table. The other benefit is that you bring others along with you in the decisions.

6. BE A STUDENT OF THE PAST

Will you take the time to document and learn not <u>what</u> you did during the pandemic but <u>how</u> you did it?

As this journey began, I shared my "why" for doing this passion project and this book. With time, our memories will certainly fade, and gone will be the valuable lessons of the two-plus years spent actively fighting Covid. If you are a business leader, please take these learnings back to your teams. I hope I inspired you to take note not of "what" you did but "how" you did it. No one wants to go through this again, yet it's important to rally your leadership teams to systematically capture your company's stories as you celebrate your accomplishments, lessons, and treasures of the pandemic.

- How did you achieve what you achieved?
- How can you scale and repeat that?
- And yes, what were the mistakes that you want to avoid in the future?

As you document your journey, remind your teams of some of the memorable, heartwarming stories and funny things that happened during Covid. All you have to do is toss out one thing like, "Remember when we left our groceries in the garage…?" and the floodgates will open.

7. THANK THE COACH

*Who helped you get to the other side of
the pandemic? Thank them!*

We discussed how there was no playbook for any of this. In listening to the many stories across the industry and countless stories from consumers, I could see that most didn't do it alone. So many across the industry put their personal lives on hold to navigate through uncharted territory.

New relationships were forged as we fumbled through the uncertainty in real time. Competitors become collaborators. Friends and family members provided trusted safe places when the seemingly unsurmountable challenges just never stopped. Restaurant managers carried unfathomable workloads as employees called out. Restaurant support center staff picked up shifts. Chain operators helped independent operators. Industry vendors and agencies provided free resources to keep businesses going.

I challenge you to think about three to five people who "coached" you and on whom you leaned during the pandemic. Make a list, then call each of them to tell them how much you appreciated their support. I promise it will bring both of you joy. It's part of the healing process that we can't forget those who supported us along this journey.

JOY IS A JOURNEY, NOT A FINAL DESTINATION.

8. LEAD WITH JOY, REASSURE WITH SAFETY

How will you "message" your customers –
knowing what to say and how to say it?

At the start of the pandemic, "lead with joy, reassure with safety" was key to unlocking the pent-up demand caused by Covid. When the doors reopened, many brands and agencies missed the mark, focusing too heavily on safety protocols instead of focusing on joy.

The Covid consumer segmentation is a reminder that even during a global pandemic, one-size-fits-all strategies don't work. Meeting consumers where they are is crucial at any time but becomes make-or-break during a pandemic. This re-entry framework was like an innovation curve – those who were excited to get to normal activities right away vs. those who were anxious and waited. Focusing on safety protocols seemed smart in the moment. Don't get me wrong: those were absolutely important to do, but it would have been best not to lead with that in messaging. The unintended consequence was that those looking for joy were turned off by those messages and those who were anxious anyway were reminded why they should stay home. How ironic, right? And we wondered why customers didn't return in droves.

We still need to lead with joy and reassure with safety. Today, it's less about fear from Covid, but now from rising violence. Joy should be center stage, yet customers are still looking for subtle safety signals. Are the lights in your parking lots all working? Do customers feel safe?

9. LOOK BEYOND THE CHALLENGES OF TODAY

How can you add value, instead of just taking price?

It's no secret that value is more than just price – it's what you get vs. what you give. Typically, that value equation just had "what you pay" as the denominator. Covid changed that. Now, our time is part of what we give.

- What you get – the food, the service, the ambiance, the total experience
- What you give – the amount of money + my time
- Was it "worth it"?

Honestly, consumers struggle with this today as too often experiences aren't that joyful. There are staffing shortages in both the front and back of house, poor training, higher prices, and oh, by the way, that favorite item that consumers came out for isn't even available. Compound that with long ticket times, and you have to ask yourself – "was it worth it?"

The pent-up consumer demand is there, but until the industry figures out this value equation, that demand will be locked up. I know what you are thinking: technology will save the day. Maybe, but our data shows that consumers are craving as many high-touch experiences as high-tech experiences. Technology should be the enabler *of* an exceptional experience, not its replacement. Again, just like price increases, technology gone too far might commoditize the brands.

Ask yourself: how can you add value, instead of just taking price? I know this sounds like motherhood and apple pie, but how much price has your brand taken in the last two years? What value have you added to offset the price?

10. CREATE JOY TO RECONNECT AND RE-ENGAGE

How will you focus on finding and delivering
more joy professionally and personally?

Fear is the opposite of joy, and it wasn't until joy was greater than fear that the economic recovery could begin. Covid divided us and took some of our humanity with it. We can't let that stand and permanently change us.

Death and tragedy often unite us as we rally together to support one another and to cope and grieve. We offer heartfelt condolences; we bring comfort and support. We bring food, and we wrap our arms around each other to get through it. I am not naïve enough to think that it's always this picture-perfect, but I choose to believe that we are inherently wired to help each other in times of need until we get in our own way with our own self-interest. The early days of Covid were no different: our country went into automatic pilot, supporting each other, and finding new ways to connect. There were countless positive examples of Americans trying to take care of each other.

It brought out the best of us but as it lingered beyond what was imaginable and the fear grew, it also brought out the worst of us.

We have to find our way back to joy in general and in business. While joy comes from within each of us, it's also the most authentic and shareable moment. It is a fleeting moment of happiness that makes us want to jump up and down.

Joy is not just something you experience alone; it comes from connecting with others. When your business delivers joy, you will win the hearts and the loyalty of your customers and employees. You will grow your share of wallet. We have to continue rebuilding and recovering from the devastation left by Covid. We are still rebuilding our economy and, honestly, we're still rebuilding ourselves.

To the industry leaders, frontline restaurant and retail workers, and everyone in between, this country owes a ton of gratitude to you for getting us to the other side.

Let the journey back to joy continue….and the business of joy.

BIBLIOGRAPHY

"31 Beautiful and Profound Joy Quotes". Spirit Button, Sept. 15, 2017. https://www.spiritbutton.com/joy-quotes/

"9/11: The Steel of American Resolve". George W. Bush Library National Archives, undated. https://www.georgewbushlibrary. gov/explore/exhibits/911-steel-american-resolve

A quote from Daring Greatly. (n.d.). https://www.goodreads.com/ quotes/884805-everyone-wants-to-know-why-customer-service-has-gone-to

Centers for Disease Control and Prevention. "CDC Museum COVID-19 Timeline," August 16, 2022. https://www.cdc.gov/ museum/timeline/covid19.html.

Davis, Krystle M. "20 Facts And Figures To Know When Marketing To Women. " Forbes, May 13, 2019 https:www.forbes.com/sites/fo rbescontentmarketing/2019/05/13/20-facts-and-figures-to-know-when-marketing-to-women/?sh=3a4704641297

Fantozzi, Joanna. "National Restaurant Association launches Restaurants Revival campaign to bring customers back to restaurants." Nation's Restaurant News, August 13, 2022. https:// www.nrn.com/restaurants-ready/national-restaurant-association-launches-restaurants-revival-campaign-bring

Gaines, Cork. "The Super Bowl Will Have 30,000 Cardboard Fans to Help the Game Look Full and Keep Real Fans Socially Distant." Insider, February 7, 2021. https://www.insider.com/super-bowl-cardboard-fans-capacity-covid-2021-2.

Google Trends. "Google's Year in Search," n.d. https://trends.google.com/trends/yis/2020/US/.

Higgins-Dunn, Noah. "Google searches for anxiety soar to record high at beginning of coronavirus pandemic, study finds." CNBC, Aug 24 2020. https://www.cnbc.com/2020/08/24/google-searches-for-anxiety-soar-to-record-at-start-of-coronavirus-pandemic-study.html

Hospitality Relief Dashboard. (n.d.). Tobin Ellis. https://www.barmagic.com/relief

Jim Rohn Quotes. (n.d.). http://www.quoteswise.com/jim-rohn-quotes-6.html

"Joy." In *The Merriam-Webster.Com Dictionary*, December 24, 2022. https://www.merriam-webster.com/dictionary/joy.

Kelly-Linden, Jordan. "Pandemic Prompts Surge in Interest in Prayer, Google Data Show." The Telegraph, May 22, 2020. https://www.telegraph.co.uk/global-health/climate-and-people/pandemic-prompts-surge-interest-prayer-google-data-show/.

Lisa W. Miller & Associates, LLC. https://www.lwm-associates.com/, linkedin.com/in/lisa-w-miller-5a53a86

McGrath, Paula. "Why Good Memories Are Less Likely to Fade." BBC News. BBC, May 3, 2014. https://www.bbc.com/news/health-27193607

Microsoft Sam. "Every Covid-19 Commercial Is Exactly the Same." YouTube, April 16, 2020. https://www.youtube.com/watch?v=vM3J9jDoaTA.

National Restaurant Association. "National Restaurant Association – The Sounds We Crave :30," August 30, 2020. https://www.youtube.com/watch?v=Bnn_AWX-qU8.

Neal Rothschild, Sara Fischer. "News Engagement Plummets as Americans Tune Out." Axios, July 12, 2022. https://www.axios.com/2022/07/12/news-media-readership-ratings-2022.

Revival Guide. (n.d.). Tobin Ellis. https://www.barmagic.com/revival

"Stephen Colbert Rude Customer Behavior - "Research Says... "." YouTube, February 17, 2022. https://www.youtube.com/watch?v=-nA8EW2JpiM.

Taylor, Kate. "Restaurants face awkward questions about how to advertise re-opened dining rooms." Business Insider, July 19, 2020 https://www.businessinsider.com/restaurants-face-questions-about-advertising-re-opened-dining-rooms-2020-7

The Difference Between Joy and Happiness. (n.d.). https://www.compassion.com/sponsor_a_child/difference-between-joy-and-happiness.htm

The White House. "Proclamation on Declaring a National Emergency Concerning the Novel Coronavirus Disease (COVID-19) Outbreak –," n.d. https://trumpwhitehouse.archives.gov/presidential-actions/proclamation-declaring-national-emergency-concerning-novel-coronavirus-disease-covid-19-outbreak/.

The White House. "Remarks by President Trump in Address to the Nation –," n.d. https://trumpwhitehouse.archives.gov/briefings-statements/remarks-president-trump-address-nation/.

WHO Director-General's opening remarks at the media briefing on COVID-19 - 11 March 2020. (2020, March 11). https://www.who.int/director-general/speeches/detail/who-director-general-s-opening-remarks-at-the-media-briefing-on-covid-19---11-march-2020

Interviews

Adams, Anita. Author Interview. Conducted by Lisa W. Miller. March and November 2022

Archer, Mike. Author Interview. Conducted by Lisa W. Miller. February 2022

Blanchette, Robin. Author Interview. Conducted by Lisa W. Miller. March 2022

Cywinski, John. Author Interview. Conducted by Lisa W. Miller. April 2022

Ellis, Tobin. Author Interview. Conducted by Lisa W. Miller. December 2022

Foster-Witherspoon, Katrina. Author Interview. Conducted by Lisa W. Miller. January 2022

Gibbons, Jack. Author Interview. Conducted by Lisa W. Miller. October 2022

Johnson, Starlette. Author Interview. Conducted by Lisa W. Miller. October 2022

Kaur, Rose. Author Interview. Conducted by Lisa W. Miller. October 2022

Landry, Sherri. Author Interview. Conducted by Lisa W. Miller. July 2022

McCarthy, Caitlin. Author Interview. Conducted by Lisa W. Miller. December 2022

McGowan, Barry. Author Interview. Conducted by Lisa W. Miller. March and November 2022

Manning, Margo. Author Interview. Conducted by Lisa W. Miller. October 2022

Nguyen, Khanh. Author Interview. Conducted by Lisa W. Miller. December 2022

Richardson, Ricky. Author Interview. Conducted by Lisa W. Miller. July 2022

Rosenberg Bittorf, Sara. Author Interview. Conducted by Lisa W. Miller. July 2022

Valade, Kelli. Author Interview. Conducted by Lisa W. Miller. February 2022

Special Thank You

Thank you to all of the following people that shared their stories with me as part of this Journey Back to Joy project:

Anita Adams, CEO, Black Bear Diner
Mike Archer, CEO, Lou Malnati's Pizzeria
Robin Blanchette, CEO & Founder, Norton Creative LLC
John Cywinski, President, Applebee's Grill and Bar
Tobin Ellis, Principal, Studio Barmagic
Jack Gibbons, CEO, FB Society Restaurant Brands
Starlette Johnson, Industry Board Director
Rose Kaur, Managing Partner, Jester&Genius
Sherri Landry, EVP, CMO, CEC Entertainment
Barry McGowan, CEO, Fogo de Chão
Margo Manning, COO, Dave & Buster's Inc.
Khanh Nguyen, CEO & Founder, ZaLat Pizza
Ricky Richardson, CEO, Eggs Up Grill
Sara Rosenberg Bittorf, Chief Strategy Officer, TGI Fridays
Kelli Valade, CEO, Denny's Corporation
Katrina Foster-Witherspoon, Head of Digital Operations, D Magazine

Thank you to a few more special people that dedicated countless hours on this project. I truly couldn't have done this without you!

Lisa Rowell
Isabel Barker
Sridharan Gunasekaran, and the team at Slide Marvels
Kelly Palmer, Daniel Rodriguez and Ken Bartholomew, and the team at Prodege, LLC

About the Author

Lisa W. Miller has spent the last three decades translating consumer data into well-integrated, actionable insights that unlock profitable sales and business growth.

Lisa is the president of a marketing, strategy, and innovation practice and a trusted advisor to C-suite executives, board of directors and private equity firms guiding and transforming their companies and capabilities. Lisa has had the opportunity to become strategic partners with many well-known and trusted global brands across varied business sectors including restaurants, consumer packaged goods, financial services, retail, healthcare, apparel, and non-profits. Prior to starting her own firm, she was Vice President Innovation at Brinker International, parent brand of Chili's Grill & Bar and Maggiano's Little Italy and Vice President Consumer Strategy & Insights at Frito-Lay/PepsiCo.

Lisa's work has been featured nationally in over 200 media interviews and speaking engagements including NBC Nightly News with Lester Holt, the Wall Street Journal, Nation's Restaurant News, Restaurant Finance Development Conference and Women's Food Service Forum Conference.

www.ingramcontent.com/pod-product-compliance
Lightning Source LLC
Chambersburg PA
CBHW071552200326

41519CB00021BB/6715